CREDO

A SHORT EXPOSITION OF CATHOLIC BELIEF

FROM THE FRENCH OF

RT. REV. A. LE ROY

BISHOP OF ALINDA
GENERAL OF THE CONGREGATION OF THE HOLY GHOST

TRANSLATED BY

E. LEAHY

FROM "NOUVELLE EDITION," 1918

EDITED BY

REV. GEO. O'NEILL, S.J., M.A.

FREDERICK PUSTET CO., (INC.)

NEW YORK AND CINCINNATI

1920

Nihil Obstat:

ARTHUR J. SCANLAN, S.T.D.
Censor Librorum

Imprimatur:

JOSEPH F. MOONEY, V.G.
Administrator

NEW YORK, *February* 15, 1919

FOREWORD

IT will be scarcely necessary to recommend a
work by Mgr. Leroy to those who have known
what his record is as a prelate of action, a
man of learning, an effective wielder of the pen.
In presenting to them and others an English
version of his book *Credo* we can offer the assurance
that it is marked by a threefold character con-
formable to that which we have just ascribed to
the author. It is a brief, pointed, business-like,
but by no means heartless, setting forth of the
entire field of Catholic Christian belief; a treat-
ment of theological problems and practical duties
in a form well calculated to meet the wants and
appeal to the judgment of the busy man or woman
of the world as we know it. Its merits of matter
and form have been fully re-created in the version
now offered to the public.

So large is the field covered by the revered
author and so precise are his details that some
slight modifications have been deemed advisable
in order to fit the work perfectly to its new circle
of readers. A few particularities have been
omitted; a few brief phrases have been expanded

in one or two passages (as that explaining the
Sixth Precept of the Church), and care has been
taken to conform the language to the latest
official declarations.

It is hoped that in its new garb the work of the
eminent French missioner and prelate will continue among Catholics and non-Catholics of the
English-speaking world the career of usefulness for
which it has been happily distinguished.

G. O'Neill, S.J.

TABLE OF CONTENTS

CONTENTS

CONTENTS

CONTENTS

CREDO

CHAPTER I

THE END OF LIFE

IF upon a desert island I were find traces of footsteps on the sand, I should say "A man has passed here." If, further on I discovered a house, I should add "He knows how to build." And if I found a sheet of paper covered with writing, I should conclude "He is intelligent, he is capable of reasoning; he writes."

Now, let us open our eyes and look round the world. Does it not reveal to you the presence of an invisible and supremely great Being? As the footsteps on the sand, the house, the page of writing, could not of themselves come into being, so the world could not of itself come into existence. To create what exists; to dispose everything in order; to give motion to the heavenly bodies; life to the plants; feeling to the animals; intelligence and conscience to man:— all this, it is quite evident, has required a first uncreated Being Whose Power is infinite, Whose mind directs everything. This great Workman, this Creator of the World, we call God, the Lord, the Most High, the Almighty.

Without Him nothing is possible; with Him everything is explained. Let Him withdraw His sustaining hand but for one hour: the sun would be extinguished; the stars would go astray; the earth would fall into ruin; life would cease; man would be annihilated. He is the necessary Being.

To take another order of ideas; — is there not within ourselves a moral law which imposes itself on our conscience and dictates to us its commands? "This act is good, do it; that act is bad, you must avoid it." It is so with all men, and so it has been throughout all time. No doubt conscience can be falsified, obscured, almost destroyed, but yet it still exists everywhere and in every one.

Now, the existence of this law, moral, universal, absolute, imposed on man by a superior independent force can only be explained by the Will of God, the Supreme and Sovereign Ruler of men.

The Ruler of men, He is also their Judge; He rewards the good; He punishes the wicked, not always in this world but of a certainty in the next, for all Eternity is His. And of necessity it must be so. For if God did not exist, or if He were for us a vague, indifferent Being, why should men trouble themselves to do that which is painful?

It is impossible to conceive that the self-sacrifice and heroic devotedness of a Francis Xavier or a Vincent de Paul, quite unrewarded (as so commonly happens) in this life, and in truth quite beyond the rewards of this life, should have no other consequence for these Saints after their death than have the useless lives of the slothful, or the crimes of the worst criminals.   If there is no God to dictate to me my duty, to punish or to reward me, to compensate for the injustice of which I am the victim, for the sorrows which overshadow my life, the anxieties which disturb me, the sacrifices which duty entails, then neither father nor mother, master nor government has sufficient authority to impose on me a duty, nor can their promises or threats suffice.   They may, indeed, impose certain acts by force, but I can resist them by force or by cunning.   And life, thus understood, would be a combat among wild beasts; would lose all its nobility.   It is impossible that this should be true.

No; man's final destiny is not decided here on earth; so much merit cannot go unrewarded; so many crimes remain unpunished; so much injustice remain without reparation.   There must be a sequel to this earthly life — there must be a God.

Many other proofs of God's existence and action might be given.   Thus, the Universe in its moral and material elements can only be explained

by one or other of the following hypotheses:
1st. It has created itself, and alone, unaided,
organized itself. 2nd. It has always existed;
it has had no beginning, and will never have an
end; it is eternal, necessary and without cause.
3rd. God has created it. The first hypothesis
is inadmissible. "If there were a moment in
which there was nothing" says Bossuet "then to
all eternity, there could have been nothing."
Let us suppose the complexity of the actual Universe represented by a series of numbers. Going
back beyond all beings, all ages, we arrive at a
point where there is nothing, and we express this
nothingness by zero. Now, it is in vain that we
multiply 0 by 0; we shall never have any other
product, that is to say, any other creation than 0.
What is this but to say that nothing can come
from nothing?

But if we cannot conceive a Universe which
of itself alone has come into existence, it is
equally irrational to imagine it as existing from
all eternity.

In the first place, such a being would be a necessary being, essentially existing of itself, and admit-
ting neither change nor imperfection nor limit —
qualities which all evidence proves our material
universe does not, can not possess.

But, on the other hand, how could the forces
or energies which govern the world be eternal?

Gradually, at every moment and everywhere, they are being changed, they become exhausted, used up, leveled down. Therefore, they are not infinite. One day they will cease, as the pendulum of a clock left to itself ceases to swing. Therefore, they had a beginning. They have been put into motion. By whom?

Moreover, in the Universe all is motion. Now, movement arises from another movement which itself arises from another, and so on in succession until we come to the initial movement. Consider once more the clock, which first of all must be made piece by piece and put together with intelligence, but the works of which will never act unless some one sets it going, and which will surely stop unless some one looks after it and winds it regularly. Well has a poet said:

> "*An independent world? I cannot understand*
> *A clock without a making, guiding hand.*"

And how shall we explain the origin of life? Life did not always exist upon the earth, for in the beginning the earth was in a state of fusion — so modern science teaches us. How has life come upon it? The same science proves to us that all that lives comes from a being living previously. The first living beings therefore must have received life from the One Who alone could give it: God. This is the history of the egg and the hen. Who made the egg? The hen. Who made the hen? The hen came from the egg. And so on to the first egg, the first hen.

No matter in what way we consider it, we must always come to the same conclusion: God is the necessary, indispensable, indisputable Being. And we have something better to do than to argue concerning His existence. Let us humble ourselves profoundly before Him as so many animated grains of dust before the sun; even if the sun is hidden by clouds, none the less do the grains of dust enjoy its light.

Further; it is thus that all nations in all ages have explained the Universe; behind the world of visible Nature they have recognized another world which we do not see, which we do not touch, but which dominates us and towards which we have duties to fulfil. "We may find" says Plutarch "towns without walls, without literature, without money, without theatre or circus; but a town without a temple, without a god, without prayer, or prophecies, or sacrifices offered to obtain what is good and to avert evil—such has never been seen, nor ever will be seen."

Travelers passing through this world, soon shall we enter by the gate of death into the next, and then our eternal destiny will be fixed according as we have lived well or ill.

Such is the end of life and its explanation. Those

who did not know this great secret may be said to have known nothing. They spent their time in eating, drinking, sleeping, in talking, in amusing themselves, in work, in suffering — and all this to no rational, satisfying end. Now, if life is only this, nothing but this, it is inexplicable; it is improbable; it is ridiculous. There must be another world in which everything is made clear, in which the truth is revealed, in which justice is reestablished.

And for this reason, if we would realize fully our destiny, we must be bound whilst here on earth to God and the next world by a sort of moral tie. This tie, these relations, this connection is the service of God, in other words Religion.[1]

A man who will not have anything to do with Religion, is a child on his way to his Father's house who takes no heed as to the road, the house, or his father.

Religion comprises: 1st. *Belief or Dogma*, that is to say, the truths which we must believe; 2nd. *Morals*, namely, the principles by which our conduct must be regulated; 3rd. *Worship*, the practises which we must observe in order to serve God.

---

[1] Religion from the Latin *re-legere* (in contradistinction to *nec-legere*, to neglect) attentive study of divine things. Others give us the etymology *re-ligare* to bind (man to God).

CHAPTER II

THE SEARCH FOR TRUTH

THE earth with all that it contains is made for man. Man is made for God, and God, being Infinite, has no other end than Himself. Made for God, man must tend towards God; this is the divinely-appointed order.

Now let us suppose a father of a family far away from his own in a rich and distant land. If he wants his children to go to him, he will not fail to point out to them the road which they are to follow; he will send them instructions; he will guide them.

God is a father. No doubt He could have given to a man a purely natural end with sufficient understanding and sufficient means to guide him in life. But, if in His goodness He has appointed to him a supernatural destiny with a share in divine goods which wholly surpass all that human beings can conceive, then He alone can provide man with the means to realize this destiny: Divine Revelation becomes absolutely necessary (Vatican Council, *De fide* II).

8

Man, on his side, by his nature is fully prepared to receive the word of God. He has intelligence, will, conscience, liberty: all these he requires with divine help to discern what is true, to recognize the good, and to follow the right road, that which will lead to his Father.

But this mysterious road, where is it? Where shall we find this Word of God, this Revelation, this Religion? And how recognize it amongst so many others which divide the world, which contradict one another, which contend for supremacy and which all alike call themselves divine?

No doubt God will have pity on men who in good faith shall have sought Him by roads not pointed out by Him — by following distorted religions, by the observance of vain practises, by accepting as good, ridiculous observances. God can never be unjust. No doubt, also, in as far as concerns us, we shall know how to practise charity towards those who are going astray. But this does not take us far enough. We have still to ask: "Is there a personal God? If this God exists, has He ordained anything? And if He has, what are the consequences of this revelation for you, for me, for every man?"

All this leads us back to our first conclusions. If God has destined us for Heaven, He cannot abandon us on earth without telling us what He requires of us. There must be found somewhere a Religion which contains integrally His Word; there must be only one, for God cannot contradict Himself. He cannot reveal to some one thing, and then to others something contradictory. God has but one word, and this Word must be the same for all His children. For all have the same nature and the same destiny.

Therefore, before all, we must seek the true Religion.

Now, the great majority of men have neither the time, nor the ability, nor the instruction necessary for this search. Clearly, God must have provided us with a means of arriving at it, a sure and easy means within the reach of all, learned and ignorant, rich and poor, gentle and simple.

But if word were to come to us that there exists somewhere a Religion which could be traced back to the very beginnings of Humanity; which had developed by being illumined by successive new lights; which could answer triumphantly all objections; which united in itself all that humanity holds as best; which would satisfy the noblest aspirations of human nature; which could even appeal to supernatural manifestations, undeniable and authenticated, such as miracles and prophecies vouchsafed as authentic proofs of its origin: — would not all this prove that such a Religion was good, was true, was divine?

And precisely an ancient and great Society does exist which fulfils all these conditions, and which with a force and clearness truly impressive claims to be the only authorized depository of the Word of God, the sole one charged to transmit it to men.

This great Society which numbers actually nearly 300 millions of members belonging to all nations and all classes, calls itself the *Catholic Church*, two words which mean the *Universal Society*. It has its head at Rome; — this Head is the Pope who is represented in all countries by Bishops, and these last in a multitude of towns and villages are themselves represented by the Catholic priests.

If this Society, which is identified with Christianity itself, has really received the deposit of Religious Truth, as it asserts, then through its means God's design is realized. It will suffice for the humblest child, as soon as it reaches the age of reason, to apply to one of the representatives of the Catholic Church to know better than any learned man what it should do in this world to reach Heaven.

Now, that the Catholic Church presents itself to us with unexceptional characteristics of truth is incontestable. With her "was seen for the first time in history the moral forces scattered amongst the traditions of the people, the good-will of upright hearts from the simplest to the most refined, the knowledge hitherto scattered amongst divers philosophies, all united by a providential inspiration in a group of intellects established hierarchically to form thus the immense community of Christian souls, and to end after three or four centuries of painful yet fruitful struggle in the triumph of a synthesis which embraces the whole of the past and illuminates the future; which at the same time has organized moral life in the world and assigned to the free action of every human being an exalted end, consoling and attainable by all; finally which has constituted for all at the confluence of all the learning of antiquity the great guiding beacon, the educating Society, the ever progressive center of light, of beneficent heat, of regulated force and devotedness, whence they should henceforth draw nobility, confidence and serenity during their earthly career" (J. Boussinesq, Revue d'Apologet., no. 238). Of all this the Catholic Church gives proofs which have never yet been refuted. According as we advance, we in our turn shall appreciate them.

Let us then, in the first place, hear the Catholic Church, whilst humbly asking of God to enlighten our reason and to touch our hearts.

"Lord" said the blind man in the Gospel "grant that I may see." This also shall be my prayer. "Grant that I may see." There are but two gates by which to enter Eternity. If I miss the right one, there remains for me but the other. Once I have passed through I shall never return. "Lord, grant that I may see the truth!"

CHAPTER III

FAITH

The Deposit of Faith — Tradition, Oral and Written — Faith and its Mysteries — The Apostles' Creed.

IF God has thus called man to a supernatural life, He is obliged to enter into relations with him whom He has created. Has He done so? "In all ages" replies Bossuet "God has created man only that He might be known and loved by him. And as He has never ceased to owe to Himself this tribute of glory and of praise, so He has never ceased throughout all ages to render it to Himself. *"Nevertheless he left not himself without testimony,"* says Holy Scripture (Acts XIV. 16). Religion must always have been on earth; it could not be otherwise, since God, at any time, could have had no other purpose. If all men have not known and loved Him, it is because they have turned aside from their right path. In every age there have been true adorers for whose sake God suffers unbelievers and continues His work.

"Where are those lovers of the Supreme and Infinite Being? We shall find them clearly pointed out in the history of one nation, the most ancient of all histories, which goes back to the first man and which manifests to us this worship of love of the One and Infinite Being which God has never permitted to be interrupted."

Now, this is precisely the teaching of the Catholic Church.

The Creator, she teaches, chose as the depositories of His Word Adam and his first sons, then the Patriarchs Noe, Job, Abraham, etc. then Moses and the Prophets of Israel. And finally He came Himself in the Person of Jesus Christ Who chose the Apostles and Evangelists to be His mouthpiece.

The assemblage of religious truths thus from the beginning revealed forms the deposit of Faith.

This deposit of Faith, in the beginning entrusted to men's memory, to be transmitted from one to the other as in a family, is what is called Tradition, a word which signifies handing or passing on. Then for their more certain preservation a number of these moral and religious teachings — the most important — were written by the inspiration of God.

These writings form the Sacred Scriptures or the Bible (from the Greek *Biblia*, books).

But neither tradition nor the Bible can be the

sole rule of our life. The Bible is not accessible to every one. It contains obscure passages; it needs to be translated into the various languages of the world, to be explained, interpreted, to be commented upon. It cannot therefore suffice for our certain guidance. For this reason God has entrusted the deposit of Faith—Tradition and the Scriptures—to the authority of the Church as our Teacher, and she it is who with God's help has been appointed to guard the deposit of Faith; to determine its true meaning, its import, its expansion; to bring it within the reach of the humblest as well as of the greatest, and to spread it amongst all mankind.

To sum up: the deposit of the Catholic Faith is composed of all the religious truths which God has revealed from the days of Adam to Saint John, the last of the Apostles. With St. John and the Book of the Apocalypse general Revelation ends. But this does not exclude those particular revelations with which God may be pleased to enrich Christian piety.

The Church can suppress nothing; can add nothing. But if she deems it fitting — to end certain controversies for instance — she has the right to define, as having been revealed or forming part of this deposit of Faith, such or such propositions. The religious truth thus recognized and proclaimed becomes henceforth a *dogma* and must be accepted by all Christians. By means of tradition we have an unbroken chain of witnesses which permit us to come into touch with Christ, and through Him with the Prophets who preceded Him and announced His coming. The deposit of the Faith is formed of this interior tradition. The Church possessed it already before the Scripture was written, and the Scripture is but an incomplete expression of it. This is why many beliefs and practises have come down to us through tradition alone — the sign of the Cross, holy water, the principal liturgical ceremonies, the number of Sacraments, the custom of baptizing infants.

With regard to Holy Scripture, it is of a two-fold character. It is at once an authentic book and worthy of belief and a doctrinal code which Holy Church holds, not as the exclusive work of man, but as one in the composition of which God has formally intervened. For this reason the Church can say that Holy Scripture has as its author God. "For the Holy Spirit has so urged and impelled these men to write it, He has assisted them in writing with supernatural grace in such a manner, that of necessity, they must conceive exactly and faithfully expose and express with infallible exactitude all that God willed that they should say, and only that which He willed" (Leo XIII, Encycl. *Providentissimus*).

But a book which the Spirit of God has inspired cannot be left to the private interpretation of the first comer.   For this reason the Church is its guardian and official interpreter.

The Bible is composed of two parts: The Old Testament[1] which includes the books written before the coming of Jesus Christ, and the New Testament, or the books written since His coming. The books of the Old Testament, about forty in number, are generally divided into three sections, according to the subjects of which they treat. The *Historical Books*, such as Genesis, Exodus, etc. which with the history of the primitive world contain that of the Jewish people chosen by God to keep His Word in the midst of the other nations, and destined to give birth to His Envoy, to the Messias, to Jesus Christ.   The *Book of Prophecy*, due especially to the four great Prophets, Isaias, Jeremias, Ezechiel and Daniel, in which are specially contained the announcement of the Coming of Jesus Christ and of His Kingdom.

The Moral Books, such as the Psalms of David, the Proverbs of Solomon, etc. whose chief end is to give precepts and counsels.

---

[1] Testament a term used to translate a Hebrew word, meaning *Alliance*, (between God and men).   The Latin translation of the books of Holy Scripture made in the 4th century by St. Jerome is called the Vulgate (*Vulgata editio* — popular edition).   It was approved of by the Church at the Council of Trent.

The New Testament, much shorter than the Old, completes and ends it by giving us the Christian Revelation, properly so called. It comprises:

The four Gospels [1] of Saint Matthew, Saint Mark, Saint Luke and Saint John, with the history of the life and the principal teachings of Jesus Christ.

The Acts of the Apostles, due to Saint Luke, the Apocalypse or "Revelation" of Saint John; The Epistles or Letters of the Apostles, — Saint Peter, Saint Paul, Saint John, Saint James, and Saint Jude. Altogether we have a collection of 72 books, composed by 40 writers in different languages (Hebrew, Syro-Chaldaic, Greek) during a period of at least 1600 years (from Moses to Saint John) without any preconcerted plan, without any possible collusion, without any sequence or preconceived idea. And we find that all these writings form a whole of marvelous unity, as if, indeed, some one throughout the sixteen centuries during which they were continued had presided over these wonderful writings. In no other religion is a similar example to be found.

These authors of the Bible, above all those of the New Testament, were, in general, men of

[1] Gospel, from the Greek εὐαγγέλιον, good news (brought to the world).

but little intellectual culture. Now, how have these writers without learning, been able to present to us in terms as simple as they are admirably appropriate, without error and without contradicting themselves or the others, truths the soundness, the coherence and the profundity of which have won the admiration of the greatest geniuses? Compared with these strange workers, philosophers and writers like Aristotle, Plato, Cicero, are but as children. It is naturally inexplicable.

One more statement: From the time that Christianity began to spread throughout the world, the books of the Old and the New Testament have been subjected to the most minute, the most learned and, often, the most prejudiced and the most insidious examination. They have been proof against all. No single objection raised against them has ever remained unanswered. Is there a book in the world which has ever been subjected to such tests?

Why have such battles been waged age after age around the Bible? Because men want to destroy the supernatural character with which it is invested; the miracles and the prophecies which it relates; the practical consequences which it imposes on private as well as public life. Vain objections! As soon as the existence of a personal and infinite God is admitted — and how can it be denied? — it is quite a simple matter to admit also that He has spoken to men; that His Word is contained in a book, and that this book is of an exceptional nature. In truth we cannot conceive Him acting otherwise.

And this applies also to the miracles and the prophecies recorded in this book. If men in power so easily make exceptions to the laws which they give us, why should not God be able to act similarly with regard to those which He has established: And if in God there is neither past nor future, if He is the "Eternal present," if in Him there is but a simple Act, indivisible and supreme, can we not see that He embraces and regulates at one and the same time the exceptions to the laws equally with the laws themselves! There is nothing more rational than a belief in miracles. And it is also one of the most natural and the most convincing proofs of truth which can be given to us.

We are not however forbidden, far from it, to take note of certain difficulties in interpretation arising from the text of the Bible, of what is in all seriousness called its "conflict" with Science. In reality, there is no conflict, except for those who wish to find such.

The whole Bible is inspired, but clearly God has not willed to make it a book of natural science. His design was to determine in its principal elements the religious and moral teaching to be given to men, especially to the children of Israel, until the definite organization of the Catholic Church. In this teaching, we find for example, the existence of one Supreme God, the Creation, the Providence of God, the unity of the human race, the organization of the Family, the command to honor God by special worship; to pray to Him; to consecrate to Him one day of the week; the promise of a future Savior etc.

Here we have the essential object of the first Revelation.

If these instructions and prescriptions are to be found here and there given with narratives and pictures of a vaguely scientific appearance, this is but an accessory element, a manner of presenting them, a popular and interesting method of fixing them in the minds of Orientals.

Before they were inspired, the biblical authors had certain natural gifts and tendencies. And it was quite natural that they should make use of them. It was quite natural also that they should write, each one in his own tongue, in his own style, in conformity with the knowledge and ideas of his time.

This simple statement suffices to do away with much of the so called "conflict."

It is now 1900 years since God, having with Jesus Christ finished all that He had to reveal to men, charged that great Society called the Catholic Church to keep His word and to spread it throughout the earth. The Catholic Church has done this. And having taught this Word of God through the course of the past ages to millions and millions of men, in Asia, in Europe, in Africa, in America, she now offers it to us: The Word of God to-day has come to our doors.

Let us open our mind and our heart to receive it. One day we shall appear before Him, and God will remind us of this.

When received by a pure, docile, simple and trustful soul, the word of God awakens Faith.[1] "Faith is a supernatural virtue, whereby, inspired and assisted by the grace of God, we believe that the things which He has revealed are true; not because the intrinsic truth of the things is plainly perceived by the natural light of reason, but because of the authority of God Himself Who reveals them and Who can neither be deceived nor deceive"[2]

No doubt, we do not understand all that Faith proposes to our belief. In Religion there are mysteries,[3] that is to say, obscure truths which are not contrary to reason but which are beyond

[1] Faith, from the Latin word *fidere*, to trust, to have confidence in some one.

[2] This is the *exact* wording and punctuation of the Vatican Council definition.

[3] From the Greek μυστήριον, a hidden thing.

it. God being infinite, transcendent, inaccessible
to our understanding, it is quite natural that we
should not grasp certain problems which relate
to His Essence, His Providence, and even to His
action in the world. But these mysteries are
not *contrary* to our reason; they are *beyond* it.
Moreover, are there not many mysteries in
Nature? "We do not know" it has been said
"the whole of anything."

Whilst we are outside a great church, the
stained-glass windows which we see above us appear coarse and ugly and their signification escapes us. Enter, and at once you will be surprised and enchanted at the beauty of their
colors and designs. They were wonders and
you never suspected it.

Some explanation, however, is here necessary,
to answer some very common prejudices. Let us
say at once: that objections against Faith only
too often are grounded on misunderstanding,
prejudice, confusion, ignorance and defiance.
Books, the reviews, the newspapers are full of
these strange blunders. A number of intelligent
men, learned, or in high places, are perfectly ignorant in the matter of Religion. In fact, if the
Catholic Religion were what it is too often represented to be, it would be our duty at once to for-
sake it. It is only by distorting it that it can be
attacked.

In the first place, "to have faith" in something is to adhere on the testimony of others to such or such truths which we cannot verify of ourselves. It suffices for us to state that the "truth" in question is not improbable and that the reliability of the testimony on which it rests is sure. All historical truths are of this nature, and even, for the generality of mankind the greater number of scientific truths.

Thus, as I believe in the existence of Alexander the Great, of Charlemagne, and of Napoleon, whom I have never seen, I may reasonably believe in the existence and actions of Jesus Christ. As I believe on the testimony of the learned scientists that the earth turns round the sun, I may believe on the testimony of that great Academy which is called the Catholic Church the whole of the religious truths which she proposes to me on the part of God, after having herself received them, studied and verified them, as His revelations.

Faith, therefore, in matters of Religion is not more contrary to reason and to science than faith in matters of history, geography or of astronomy.

Further, no more than between Science and the Bible, can there be any real conflict between Science and Religion. For Science and Religion have the same Author; they are two different, but not contrary, aspects of the divine revelation of Truth which is one. Consequently, when one is in seeming contradiction to the other, we should wait and inquire; then we shall discover either that the conflict is imaginary, or that the theory which engenders it is in itself wholly or partially erroneous. What is true according to reason, according to Faith cannot be false, and *vice versa*.

Thus, it would be very wrong to reproach Faith with being contrary to the independence and freedom of the understanding. If, as we maintain, Faith is one aspect of the Truth, by enlarging and exalting the domain of the understanding it does not limit it. Certainly, as soon as we know that a thing is true, we are no longer free to deny it; the understanding is limited by the very limits of Truth itself. According to the argument of our objector, the most ignorant mind is the freest, the most primitive negroes of central Africa are the most perfect free-thinkers, their understanding being independent of all truth, astronomical, physical, chemical, philosophical, historical and religious.

If Faith circumscribes the Kingdom of Truth, it at the same time extends it.

Innumerable are the *savants* who have been believers; in his researches and his aspirations not one of these has ever been hampered by his Faith; on the contrary it has been to all a precious assistance and the source of fresh knowledge.

After all, the whole question is whether God

exists, whether He is All-powerful, all good, whether He has spoken to Humanity. For, if He has done so, we must respond to His voice. What reasonable man could refuse to accept His word?

Between religious faith and scientific faith, there are, however, essential differences.

In the first place, by scientific Faith I *know* and I adhere to the truth, having regard only to the veracity of the witnesses. In religious Faith I really *believe*, by humbly submitting myself to God, as soon as I know that He has spoken. This is an act of the understanding, of the will, determined besides by divine grace.

In reality, Faith is a supernatural gift or grace from God, but a supernatural grace which He refuses to none, provided that they bring to it the necessary dispositions; for it is also a virtue, involving on our part a certain effort. Therefore, if we wish to acquire it, we must begin by removing the obstacles to faith—pride, sensuality, heedlessness, indifference, the preoccupations of an inferior and human order, and seek God with courage, simplicity and loyalty. We must not oppose Truth. It is not by mere exercise of the understanding that we arrive at it. God requires the whole man, and that is why man should go to God with his whole mind and with his whole heart.

Hence, hand in hand with those who are qualified to act as our guides, let us advance with humility and confidence, "as unto a light that shineth in a dark place, until the day dawn, and the day-star arises in your hearts" (Epist. St. Pet., II, 1, 19).

The Catholic Church has summed up its Faith in a brief formula which is called the *Creed, the Symbol of the Apostles*, or the *Profession* of the Christian Faith.[1] It is as follows:

I believe in God, the Father Almighty, Creator of heaven and earth. And in Jesus Christ, his only Son, our Lord; who was conceived by the Holy Ghost, born of the Virgin Mary, suffered under Pontius Pilate, was crucified, died, and was buried; he descended into hell; the third day he rose again from the dead; he ascended into heaven, and sitteth at the right hand of God, the Father Almighty; from thence he shall come to judge the living and the dead. I believe in the Holy Ghost, the Holy Catholic Church, the communion of Saints, the forgiveness of sins, the resurrection of the body, and the life everlasting. Amen.

[1] From *Credo*, Latin word which means "I believe," *Symbol*, that is to say, an abridgment (of the truths taught by the Apostles, and which we must believe).

CHAPTER IV

CATHOLIC BELIEF

God, Providence, the Blessed Trinity

GOD is the necessary Being.

Who could have made heaven and earth if God had not created them? Who could have set the planets in motion, assigning to each one its place? How can any one be an atheist, beholding the vault of Heaven studded with stars, so many thousands of worlds revolving in the infinite distances of space?

Whence came the order, the life, everywhere to be found on the earth, from the most minute organisms of which millions are contained in a glass of water, to the most varied forms of plant life, from animal life of every kind to Man? As well say that the Cathedral of Paris in one night of itself sprang into being by the drifting together of the stones, the sand, the dust. As well say that on the railways the locomotives were constructed by chance, and of themselves began to draw the carriages without any guiding hand. As well say that the letters of the alphabet formed themselves into groups, and of themselves composed the books in our libraries. As well say all this, as say that the Universe was formed by chance.

The Universe is a work of art; consequently it is the work of an Intelligence. Hence all nations believe in a God. And conscience itself, does it not speak to us interiorly, as a voice which God has placed within us?

Voltaire, who, that he might not have to practise it, was the blind, prejudiced enemy of Christianity, firmly believed in God, Whom after Plato, he calls "the eternal geometrician." One of the proofs which he gives of the existence of God is to be remembered; it is as follows: "People," he writes "tell you confidently that the combination of this universe was possible, since it exists. Therefore it was possible that it was arranged by motion." And to this Voltaire makes answer: "Take four planets only, Mars, Venus, Mercury and the earth. At first let us think of nothing but the place where they are, abstracting all the rest, and let us see what the probabilities are that motion alone (occasioned by chance) will place them in their respective positions (which they must occupy or general destruction will result). We have but twenty-four chances in this combination, that is to say that it is twenty-four to one that these planets will not be found where they are (and where they must be) on account of their relation one to the other.

"Let us add to these four planets Jupiter and then Saturn. Afterwards take all the secondary planets, all their combinations, all their movements, all the beings which vegetate, which live, which feel, think, act on these planets; you obviously increase the number of possibilities. Multiply this number for all eternity until it reaches what our weakness calls *infinite*, there will be always a single chance in favor of the formation of the world — as it is by mere motion (accidental); therefore, it is possible that in all eternity the mere motion (accidental) of matter may have produced the whole universe."

Now, for two reasons this supposition seems tremendously chimerical: "The first is that in this universe there are intelligent beings, and that you cannot prove that intelligence could be produced by mere motion.

"Second, that on your own showing it is to wager *infinity* against one that an intelligent constructive cause animates the universe." (X. Moisant, Psychologie de l'Incroyant, p. 15, Paris, Beauchesne.)

In other terms, chance, which is a blind force, unconscious, fatal, — one should say non-existent — can only produce chaotic results.

Now the order which with a view to an end as-

signs to everything its own place, evidently supposes intelligence. And when this order extends
to the whole universe in its entirety and its smallest details, the intelligence which has willed this
order, has realized it, and maintains it, can only
be Infinite Intelligence.

Without God, nothing is possible, without God
nothing could be.

This question of the existence of God lies at the
basis of everything. The Vatican Council de-
fines it in the following terms "Holy Church holds
and teaches that by the natural light of human
reason and by means of created things, God, the
beginning and end of all things, may be known
with certainty. For, since the creation of the
world, the intelligence of men by means of the
beings which God has created had perceived His
invisible perfections. Nevertheless God in His
wisdom and goodness has been pleased to make
revelation of Himself and to reveal the eternal
decrees of His will in another way — the supernatural way. This is what the Apostle tells us:
'God, Who at sundry times and in divers manners
spake in time past unto the fathers by the prophets
hath in these last days spoken to us by *his* Son
. . .'" (Hebr. VI. 1–2).

God is not *unknowable*, for we know that He
exists, but He is incomprehensible to our understanding because He is infinite; *infinite*, that is to

say, He cannot be limited by time nor space, nor matter nor any imperfection whatsoever, by any power, any force, any law. He is supremely above all things, and we can only speak of Him in a very imperfect manner, whilst seeking the reflection of His attributes or qualities in man or in the world, that is to say, in His Works. Happily He has revealed Himself to us, and hence it is that we know by revelation many things about Him which reason confirms, but which of its own powers it could not have discovered.

In the first place the best definition of God is given by Himself in the Bible. "I Am Who Am." He said to Moses (Exod. III. 14). This is the meaning of the Hebrew word Jahweh, which has been rendered Jehovah. He is. He is unequaled and Infinite, consequently eternal without beginning and without end, without past or future, beyond time, which had its beginning in Him, which passes and which must end. He is a Spirit, a pure Spirit, without body or shape or form of any kind, penetrating matter without being penetrated by it, infinitely powerful, infinitely free, infinitely just, infinitely good.

Let us understand these things well. God is. He is everywhere; He knows everything; He sees everything; He knows me personally, and now, at this very moment in which I am thinking of Him, He is here.

But God being a spirit, He remains invisible to our eyes. So on foggy days does the sun reveal itself but by a pale light, and he who had never seen it shining in a clear sky, could not from this mere reflection form to himself an idea of its splendor.

Therefore, if we speak sometimes of "the eyes of God" of "the arm of God," it is only by comparison and to make His action in the world better understood, and it is in the same spirit that the Father is represented by the figure of an aged man, the Son by that of a man, and the Holy Spirit by that of a dove.

After having created the world, God preserves it and governs it in the whole and in detail. Thus God is not a personification more or less vague of the general equilibrium, an inaccessible power, a kind of remote and solitary monarch. He is a God ever present to the conscience of him who will indeed hear Him, He is a God of Love, of Wisdom, of Holiness. He is a compassionate God, just, merciful, good. And for this reason we also call Him Providence: He *provides;* He watches over all; He thinks of all; He is attentive to all. It is not that the government of the world gives Him any trouble. Everything is present to God by one sole idea as on the dial of an immense clock — God does not foresee, He sees. But, some one will say, how reconcile this action of Providence with man's free will. For the catechism tells us that "nothing happens in the world except by the order or permission of God." That is certain. And that man is free is also certain. These are, says Bossuet the two ends of the chain which we hold in our hands without indeed seeing how the links are joined towards the middle. But do we want to know so much? We are passing through life as a sailor passes in a ship over the Ocean; God's breeze blows more or less strongly; we can unfurl a sail and let ourselves be driven; we can also choose the direction in which we would go, to the right, to the left, or even against the wind. Are we not then free, and does the breeze which carries us along deprive us of our free will?

Another difficulty is the problem of moral and physical evil in the world. God did not create evil, for He is the supreme Good, but having given to the angels and to man freedom to commit it, in order to try them and to permit them to acquire merit, He has not willed to withdraw this freedom from them. This, no doubt is a great mystery. But we have scarcely a right to call God to account and to ask His reasons. What are we on this little earth where we fret ourselves in the darkness? What vanity to wish to reduce everything to the level of our own personality! It is the whole of Creation, it is the general harmony, which must serve as the rule by which to judge the details or the accidents of the beings of this world. Man forms part of the universe; hence he is subject to the laws which govern the universe. By taking this point of view, which is the true one, the Saints, instead of giving way to useless complaining, were always humbly submissive to the adorable will of God.

God alone knows the reason of all things. He is supremely independent in the distribution of things, and we only know that in no case can He commit any injustice whatsoever.

Evil is a thing essentially negative, it is the privation of good. For the non-existence of evil in the world it would be necessary that the world should be perfect, like God Himself. Now, there is a contradiction between these two terms: *created* and *perfect*. Nothing created can be absolutely perfect.

God does not directly will physical evil. But God permits it to be produced as an effect of the laws generally established, with a view to a more elevated order which God alone knows.

With regard to moral evil, God does not will it directly or indirectly; it is the act of free, rational beings, and to suppress it would necessitate depriving them of their freedom. God represses it in this world or in the next and makes it, in any and every case, subservient to the accomplishment of His sovereign Will.

In conclusion, let us say with Fénelon "The whole alone is intelligible, and the whole is too vast to be looked at close at hand."

But it is St. Paul who gives us the true and definite answer: "For I reckon that the sufferings of this time are not worthy to be compared with the glory to come, that shall be revealed in us." (Romans VIII, 18, 23).

What we see here on earth is only the beginning; it is in the next world that all ends and all is explained; there it is that all injustice is repaired, that all sorrows are forgotten, that merit is rewarded, and that each one receives what is due to him. And thus in the presence of evil in this world we find a fresh proof of a necessary reparation which is brought about for us in Eternity.

"O the depth of the riches of the wisdom and of the knowledge of God! How incomprehensible are his judgments, and how unsearchable his ways!

For who hath known the mind of the Lord? Or who hath been his counsellor?

Or who hath first given to him, and recompense shall be made him?

For of him, and by him, and in him, are all things: to him be glory forever. Amen." (St. Paul, Rom, XI.)

"There is no God but (God)" say the Mussulmans. And they are right. But through Revelation we know that in God, Who is One in nature, substance or essence, there are three persons, distinct yet eternally coexistent, coequal and indivisible, to whom have been given the names of the Father, the Son and the Holy Ghost.

This is the mystery of the Blessed Trinity. We do not say: Three Gods make one God, or that three and one are in God one and the same thing. That would be absurd; *one* is always one, *three* are always three. We say: the three divine Persons, coexistent in the same nature, are distinct in personality. In other terms the three Persons in God represent three distinct ways in which one sole substance subsists. In this there is no contradiction.

For example, consider the sun; the source, the light and the heat form but one sun. In one triangle there are three angles. The human soul is at one and the same time intelligence, sensibility and will.

No doubt $1 + 1 + 1 = 3$, but $1 \times 1 \times 1 = 1$. And the divine Persons are not added to each other, if one may speak so, to form the Infinite. It is the Infinite Himself Who is multiplied in one single Act, one single Thought, one sole Love. And it is this triple relation which is the Trinity.[1]

[1] Trinity, that is to say Three in One, One in Three (Trina Unitas). The word *Person* has not here the usual meaning given to it of designating distinct and separate individualities. Granted that the divine Essence is one and infinite, the Father is this Essence inasmuch as

But these are only very imperfect comparisons. God alone can know Himself. All that we can understand is that there is no contradiction in what He has revealed to us of His nature.

Even this revelation has only been indirectly suggested, indicated and represented in the Old Testament, no doubt from a fear that the idea of one only God in the ill-cultivated minds of the people might be changed. But in the New Testament it is clear and precise; in many places there is question of the Heavenly Father, of the Eternal Word or Son of God, and of the Holy Spirit, the Paraclete or Consoler.

it engenders the Son, the Son is this Essence inasmuch as it is engendered by the Father; the Spirit is this Essence inasmuch as it proceeds from the Father and from the Son. And these three relations of *paternity*, of *filiation* and of *procession* are what constitute the three divine Persons or the Blessed Trinity.

CHAPTER V

THE CREATION

The Angels — The Material World — Man

I N the beginning God created heaven, and earth." With these words begins the first Book of Holy Scriptures, that called Genesis.[1] By this we are to understand that at a given moment which was the beginning of time, God produced all that exists outside Himself. He spoke, and all was made: Heaven and earth, things visible and invisible.

In creating the world He gave to it rules and laws, according to which it moves, like an admirable machine all the details of which have been foreseen and pre-arranged.

Was the creation of this world a sudden or a gradual effect of the Creator's power, or was it the result of the evolution of insensible and long protracted successive developments under the directing action of the Most High? To what epoch does it in its different parts go back? What

---

[1] Γένεσις, in Greek, the beginning.

is the age of the world, of the first plants, the first animals, the first man? Of all this we can think whatever may seem to us the most probable, without coming into conflict with traditional interpretations and the decisions of the Church. We know, in any case, that neither matter, nor spirit, nor movement, nor order, nor life can have had a beginning without God.

In the narrative of Genesis we are indeed told that God created all things in six days and that on the seventh day He rested. But the greatest latitude is allowed to us in giving this expression every meaning compatible with the essential fact which the sacred writer had in view — that God is the Creator of Heaven and earth. The Hebrew word expressed by "days" might signify "epochs" of undetermined length in the course of which the various parts of the Creation came into being. And in this the Bible does not differ from Science.

The first beings created by God were the angels.[1] All were created good, but free — free to make use of their intelligence and their will to direct them to God or to turn away from Him. Now, some with Michael [2] at their head remained faithful to their Creator and were eternally rewarded. They enjoy the sight of the Eternal God;

[1] *Angel* — in Greek ἄγγελος, messenger.
[2] Meaning in Hebrew: *Who is like unto God?*

they execute His orders and watch over nations and individuals. To each of us is assigned a Guardian Angel, whose presence should inspire us with reverence.

The others, led away by Lucifer or Satan [1] rebelled against God. But immediately they fell into Hell, and were fixed in evil, as the others were fixed in good. However a certain activity is left to them, and they use this to try to make us fall into sin, to induce us to offend God and so be lost eternally with them. They are called bad angels, evil spirits, devils or demons. Both angels and demons alike are spirits without bodies or form. The pictures which we see of them are merely intended to give us some idea of them.

When everything on earth had been prepared to receive them, God made the first man and the first woman: first the man, whose body, says the Scripture, was made of the slime of the earth, and then the woman, who was taken from the body of man — to show that both, being of the same substance, should be united in mutual affection.

And God breathed into both "the breath of life" capable of knowing, of reasoning, of willing,

---

[1] *Lucifer*, that is to say, *light-bearer*. *Satan*, from a Hebrew word signifying *adversary*, *rebel*; *devil*, from a Greek word meaning detractor; *demon* has the sense of a *spirit* (bad).

of discerning and choosing between good and evil; this is the *human soul* which is a spirit, an immortal spirit. When, indeed, death comes to separate the soul from the body, this body becomes rapidly decomposed, but the soul being immaterial cannot become decomposed like a piece of flesh; it returns to God Who judges it whilst awaiting the general resurrection of the dead. For every child that comes into existence God creates a soul.

The first man was called Adam and the first woman Eve.[1] All men, white, yellow, black, red, free men or slaves, great or lowly, civilized or savages are descended from this first family. All therefore are brothers, and should like brothers help one another.

Such is the Catholic doctrine regarding our origin. It is summed up in these few words: The creation by God in the beginning of time of all things; the formation of man's body from preexistent matter—"the slime of the earth" says the Bible: the special creation of the human soul, "the spirit or breath of life"; the unity of the human race.

Now not only does natural or philosophical science not contradict this teaching of our Faith; it fully confirms it.

[1] *Adam*, in Hebrew signifying *red* earth; *Eve*, that is to say *Life*, (in Greek Zoe).

It is scarcely necessary to demonstrate that the hypothesis of evolution or transformism, by which certain adversaries thought they could suppress God, on the contrary supposes Him necessary.

If man descended from an ape or some other animal, who made that ape or other animal? Whence came life? Whence came matter? Spontaneous generation is a fiction, and evolution can only be a continued creation by a Supreme Power and Intelligence.

The truth is that the whole Creation represents as it were an immense and magnificent hierarchy in which are ranged harmoniously:—matter in its different states (gaseous, liquid and solid); plants from the most rudimentary forms to the most perfect; animals in their species nearest to plants and to man; man, a rational animal who in himself alone forms a separate category; and finally, angels, pure spirits whose mysterious choirs continue this upward movement into Heaven to the presence of the Creative and Supreme Power Who in His infinite Majesty dominates all.

In this universal ascending scale of creatures, the distinguishing characteristic of man is — we have just pointed it out — that he is *"a reasoning animal,"* composed of a body and of a soul. This soul sets him apart in a rank altogether his own. If indeed this soul unites in itself all the vital forces of plants and animals, — in a lower plane vegetable or nutritive life, and in a middle plane animal or sensitive life—in a superior plane it is characterized by spiritual life which sets between it and the other visible creatures an impassable gulf. It is from this soul man has intellectual light by which he grasps the immaterial, reasons, draws conclusions, possesses an articulate language and makes progress; it gives to him free will which permits him to choose between good and evil, and makes of him a moral being; finally, by it he has religious feeling, which causes him to turn naturally to his last end which is God. These characteristics which are common to all men, however backward they may be, and which are absolutely unknown in animals, no matter to what degree of perfection they may have been brought, ensure to man authority over Creation and prove that he has been made to reign over the earth.

The soul of man is united to his body without being localized in such or such a part; it is, for example, like light which penetrates glass.

No doubt we understand that we have a soul; it obtrudes itself on us; its action is familiar to us. But how are we to prove scientifically its existence? Let a great *savant*, Claude Bernard, answer.

"The human body" he says "is composed of substances which are continually renewed. All the parts of the body are subjected to a perpetual movement of transformation. Each day you lose a little of your physical being, and you replace by food what you lose. So that in a period of about eight years your flesh, your bones are replaced by new flesh, new bones which by degrees have been substituted by means of these successive alluvions. The hand with which you write to-day is not at all composed of the same molecules as eight years ago. The form is the same but it is fresh substance which fills it. And what I say of the hand I say of the brain. Your cranial box to-day is not filled with the same cerebral matter that filled it eight years ago. If, then, in eight years everything in your brain changes, how does it happen that you remember perfectly the things you saw, heard, or learned eight years ago? If these things, as certain physiologists maintain, are lodged, incrusted in the lobes of your brain, how is it that they survive the disappearance of these lobes? These lobes are not the same which you had eight years ago, and yet your memory has retained intact its deposit. There must be then something more than matter in man, something immaterial, permanent, ever present, and independent of matter. That something is the soul."

CHAPTER VI

THE NATURAL ORDER AND THE SUPERNATURAL ORDER; THE FALL AND THE REDEMPTION

WHAT we have said of God and of Creation leads us to another great truth.

Beyond this world in which we are living for the present there is another world for which we are destined. This explains to us why it is that men of every race all over the earth and in every age appear to us as beings essentially religious. Everywhere man raises his eyes above his horizon; he renders his homage to the Author of the Universe; he calls to his assistance the invisible Powers, and at his death he feels that through his soul he penetrates into "a land beyond the grave." How could this belief have taken hold of the human race if it had not been founded on, and sustained by numerous clear, incontestable facts? "If there had never been anything of all this," says Pascal, "it is impossible that men could have imagined it, and still more impossible that so many others should have believed it."

There are insects the larvae of which live in water; this is the first phase of their existence, and when it is ended their wretched body is transformed; they develop brilliant wings, and we behold them flying from flower to flower in full daylight.

We are somewhat like these insects. Above the marshes of this present life we surmise that there is another world illumined by the eternal Sun, and we aspire to be transformed there and delivered from all our miseries.

Now as there exist Nature and a world above Nature we may suppose similarly a natural order or state and a supernatural order or state.

In the natural order man would be provided with all the means due to his *nature* as man to attain his natural end: to feed himself; to maintain his race; to improve himself; to develop his intelligence; to ameliorate his lot; and even to arrive at the knowledge of God.[1] In addition to this the supernatural order comprises the gifts, the favors, the helps superior to the nature of man which are not due to him, without which he can live, eat, sleep and act intelligently and freely, but which from pure goodness God grants to him that he may be enabled to attain to the

---

[1] In reality, this purely natural state has never existed, man, from his creation or shortly after, having been raised to the supernatural state from which he afterwards fell.

end of his supernatural destiny — union by the Beatific Vision with his Creator in Heaven for all eternity. The whole of these lights, of these forces, and these invisible beauties uplift our nature and establish it in what is called on earth the supernatural state or state of grace and in Heaven the state of glory.[1]

These few explanations will help to the better understanding of what follows.

The world as we know it, with the admirable laws which govern it in its whole and in its innumerable details, with the life circulating upon it, with its multiplied families of plants and of animals, existed long before the appearance of the human race.

The hour appointed by Providence came. God created the rational free animal who alone on earth could know Him, love Him and serve Him, and later be united more perfectly with Him in eternity.

This was Man.

What was the exact, external appearance of this first representative of our race we know not. But we can, in the first place, assert positively that he was provided with all the faculties of body and mind which were necessary to him in order to realize his end. Further, Holy Scripture

[1] Grace is so called because it is a favor *graciously or benevolently granted* by God to man.

teaches us that man, coming from the hands of God, was raised to a supernatural state of grace and holiness which caused his soul to live with a divine life and permitted him to attain his destiny of eternal felicity. God crowned this grace by rendering man impassible and immortal, immune from concupiscence, ignorance, infirmity and death.

In these conditions, man turned towards God as the compass turns to the Pole.

But God willed that man, being created free, should have the merit of himself determining his lot and that of his race. He gave him therefore a commandment which would prove his fidelity, make clear to his conscience the moral Law, and assure happiness to him forever on earth and in Heaven.

Alas! man made use of his free will not for the gaining of merit, but for his own destruction. By the threefold sin of pride, disobedience, and sensuality, he turned away from God and from his supernatural end; he turned to all that was opposed to that end; to the enemy of all good.

At the same time he lost the grace which sanctified his soul, as well as his immunity from concupiscence, ignorance, sorrow and death; he fell to the state of a creature still intelligent and free, but ungrateful and rebellious, that is to say, sinful; as far as concerned the supernatural life, it was the death of the soul, and consequently the loss of the glorious life with God. This is what is called the Fall or Original Sin.

Of this the beginning of our history, Genesis gives a striking account. God, says the sacred writer, having created Adam and Eve to His image and likeness in a state of Justice and Holiness, He placed them in the garden of Eden,[1] and He said to them "Of every tree of paradise thou shalt eat: but of the tree of knowledge of good and evil, thou shalt not eat. For in what day soever thou shalt eat of it, thou shalt die the death." Then the serpent (under whose form we must recognize the devil) said to the woman "No, you shall not die the death. For God doth know that in what day soever you shall eat thereof, your eyes shall be opened; and you shall be as Gods, knowing good and evil." The woman, thus tempted, looked at the forbidden fruit, saw that it was good, took it and ate of it, and gave it to the man who ate of it also.[1]

Immediately their eyes were opened and they understood the enormity of their sin.

And God made Himself heard. He cursed the serpent, and told the woman the miseries which would be hers; He condemned the man, doomed henceforth to live and till an unwilling soil, to eat his bread in the sweat of his brow, "till thou

[1] Eden signifies delights. It is called the terrestrial Paradise.

return to the earth" said the Lord "out of which thou wast taken: for dust thou art, and into dust thou shalt return."

Adam, whom God had constituted our Head, bore in himself all Humanity, and with him all Humanity fell. He lost, in effect, the privilege of transmitting to his descendants the supernatural and preternatural gifts which he had himself lost; his children would be born in the same state of slavery into which he had allowed himself to fall. But these latter are not *personally guilty* — nor could they be — of a fault of which they have only incurred the guilt through their relation to their father.

The original fall, therefore, is essentially the state of privation of sanctifying grace or supernatural life in the human soul, as a result and consequence of the personal sin of Adam, our common father, — a privation entailing a certain degradation of our whole being. Accidentally and secondarily it is also the loss of the precious immunities with which Adam and Eve had been favored. Consequently:

1. Original Sin does not imply any injustice on the part of the Creator. It would be otherwise, if by this default our nature had been radically perverted, and rendered incapable of all good, as Luther thought; but this is a condemned error.

2. Original Sin in us is not a sin of the will,

but a sin of nature, inherent in the nature and transmitted with the nature.

3. In giving birth to children, parents communicate original sin to them only by causing them to be born in the state of fallen nature in which they are themselves.

4. Children who die without Baptism are deprived of the sight of God, but we are quite free to believe that in the other world they are not subject to any corporal punishment and can enjoy a certain natural happiness.

5. Finally this Christian dogma could not be demonstrated experimentally by the actual state of our nature and the presence of evil in the world. It is only through Revelation that it has become known to us; and, freed from the errors and exaggerations with which it is sometimes surrounded, it contains nothing contrary to sound reason. However with Pascal, it may be said "The enigma of our condition has its twists and folds in this mystery, in such a manner that without this mystery man is more inconceivable, than this mystery is inconceivable to man."

If Adam's posterity had remained forever separated from their Creator without any relation to the real and final destiny for which God had intended them, the end which He proposed to Himself in the Creation of Man would (we may say) have been a failure.

God did not will that His designs should be thus defeated. And for this reason the Redemption of the human race accomplished by the Incarnate Word was designed to give us the means of regaining here on earth sanctifying grace and in the next world its fruition which is eternal life, with all the immunities lost by our first parents. The Fall, in truth, must have its correlative reparation. Reparation is the divine consequence of the Fall.

CHAPTER VII

OUR first parents, deprived of that supernatural life and those exceptional privileges with which they had been endowed, immediately comprehended the enormity of their fault. Confounded, repentant, but cut off from their Creator, what was to become of them? The good things which had been entrusted to them, and which they were to bequeath to their descendants, had been wasted, lost; was it to be so forever?

God, when cursing the infernal serpent, said to him "I will put enmities between thee and the woman, and thy seed and her seed: she shall crush thy head and thou shalt lie in wait for her heel." (Gen. III. 15.) Thus, was the offspring of the woman to be at feud with the offspring of the serpent, that is to say: the human Race in the person of the Savior and those who shall belong to Him the Savior, born of the woman, shall bruise the serpent's head; but the serpent

shall retain sufficient life to inflict cruel injury
on the human race, and by the evil which he shall
do to it, he will more than once bite its heel. The
whole history of the world is contained in these
words, first heard at the beginning of the ages.

The fault has been committed, but already the
words of pardon are spoken. To this mysterious
Savior thus promised to us are henceforth attached all our destinies. He is the magnificent
link between God whence He comes and Humanity with which, that He may redeem it, He
must be clothed. We shall be told His title:
"*Emmanuel, God with us.*"

By promising to men this Reconciler who was
"to take away the sins of the world," God turned
back to them. He directed their aspirations
towards the Ideal, and at the same time He armed
them against the evil which they must labor to
crush under foot: a suggestive image which
shows us the guiding line which man is to follow — to trample on our evil instincts and to
fix our gaze on high, on Truth, on Good.

Felix culpa! Happy fault, cries out the Catholic
Church in her liturgy of Holy Saturday "which
obtained for us such a Redeemer."

The first children of Adam and Eve were Cain
and Abel. By degrees families were organized,
then tribes, then nations; ever more and more
the earth was peopled, and language, habits and

customs, the external aspects of various races began to assume their respective characteristics.

When dispersing, men carried away with them a common religion with the promise of the future Savior. This was the primitive religion. It consisted of these essential elements: Belief in God as the Author of the World, the Sovereign of the Universe, the Father of men, the Master of Life and Death. The survival of the human soul after death. The distinction between good and evil; between lawful and unlawful things; between the sacred and the profane. The conception of sin and its expiation. The necessity of prayer, of offerings and of sacrifice. The organization and maintenance of families. The expectation of a future Savior.

Thus, doing good according to the knowledge which they had of it, men could save their souls by corresponding with God's grace.

Unhappily a sort of counterfeit religion, magic,[1] was not long in springing up; it set up in opposition to the Priesthood, to Belief, to morality, and to the worship of the true God sorcerers, secret societies, magic rites, malefic practises, and all that mass of superstition and of practises called pagan, which have for their object inanimate

---

[1] By this name, is meant here the mass of mock-religious practises by which it is claimed that the invisible powers can be forced to give what is asked.

creatures, the planets, the souls of the dead, spirits, and even the devil himself, and which, becoming mixed up with the primitive religion, have distorted it, and even rendered it unrecognizable. Such is the miserable condition in which at the present day we find whole populations of inferior civilization in Africa and in other parts of the world.

The mists which enshroud those distant ages defy penetration. We only know from the Scripture that at a certain epoch, one race, that of Seth, was chosen to be the guardian of the Truth; that when this race itself became corrupted, God purified the earth whereon it dwelt by submerging it beneath a great flood which is called the Deluge; that from this flood the just Noe with his family escaped in the Ark which he had built. Noe had three sons, Sem, Cham, and Japhet, the traditional ancestors of the Semitic, Hamitic and Aryan families.

Later on, at a date which History is beginning to determine in a manner more or less vague, there arose those old civilizations of which traces are found to-day in Asia Minor, in India, in China, in Egypt, in Greece, in Rome, and each of which practised a particular religion with the superstitions which characterized it.

At the same time to keep always intact the Truth, to insure the preservation of His Word in its integrity, to recall the primitive promises, and to prepare for the coming of the Savior, God chose from the posterity of Sem a family in Chaldea of which Abraham was the Head. Abraham begot Isaac, who begot Jacob or Israel, and Jacob had twelve sons who were the ancestors of the twelve tribes which formed the Jewish or Hebrew people. All these ancients are called the Patriarchs, that is to say, the heads of the ancient families.

It was from this people, who at that time merited the name of "the people of God," that God raised up Moses, to whom He gave His written Commandments, and who organized the Jews into a nation. After Moses came the Prophets[1] charged at intervals more or less prolonged to recall to the people the true Religion and the future coming of the Savior.

At last in the fulness of time God sent Him Whom He had promised from the beginning, Whom so many generations of men had expected and Who came to bring peace to men of good will, Our Lord Jesus Christ.

Such is in summary the history comprised in the Old Testament. In surveying this long tract, concerning certain stages of which we have no precise information, we see at once that in all

---

[1] Prophet (Greek, $\pi\rho o\phi\eta\tau\eta s$) a man inspired of God in what he says or announces.

ages man appears therein as a religious being. Separated often by seas, by immense continents, by different tongues, by a civilization more or less advanced, by contrary interests, everywhere men are organized into families under the protection of sacred laws; everywhere the son of Adam prays; he hopes; he expects. Feeling that he is in this world as a stranger, a traveler, a lodger, he pays his rent to the Supreme Master who has placed him in it by offerings and sacrifices, figures of and preparations for the great sacrifice of Redemption which was promised, and which is destined one day to replace them over the whole inhabited earth.

But simultaneously with this reflection there arises another.

This man, let him give way ever so little to his own inspirations regarding Religion and Morality, falls into strange errors. The more even, one would say, that he advances in material civilization the more he becomes the sport of his imagination, of his pride, of all his passions: in the East, in Greece, in Rome did not the progress of literature, of science, of art, of luxurious living, go hand in hand with the vilest corruption? Thus Humanity had full opportunity to show of what, by itself, it was capable. To preserve and guide it Humanity requires God's Hand.

And this God has done. After having entrusted

to the first man a Belief, a Morality, a Worship, that is to say, a Religion consisting of some essential elements — those which we have enumerated and which are found everywhere, even now, — He assures its preservation by choosing men, families, and finally a people whom He made the depositories and the guardians of His instructions and His promises.

Man's nature being everywhere the same, and everywhere religious, it is not surprising that all religions resemble one another in certain points. These analogies, doctrinal or ritual, far from constituting an objection to Christianity, are explained conformably to their ideas. The innumerable forms of Protestantism all retain, intermingled with their errors, something of the Catholic Religion. Similarly Animism (which gives a soul to inanimate objects), Fetichism (which invests images or idols with mysterious power), Polytheism (which multiplies its gods), Pantheism (which identifies the Deity with the Universe): all these so called Religions are the heresies of the first, the only and the real Religion.

In other words, the great stream of Humanity since its origin has always been as a current of pure water, which, unfortunately, as it moves along gathers on its surface flotsam coming from every side. But the water is still derived from a pure source and remains genuine and pure. In the same way the Primitive, Patriarchial, Mosaic and Christian Religion, under the one name of the Universal or Catholic Religion, moves along with Humanity itself, and claims as its own all that is true and all that is good. All else it rejects. Here we have the explanation of how it is that all religions resemble one another, at least in some of their elements. And for this reason also, it can be said that outside the true Religion, the religions have nothing of their own save their errors.

CHAPTER VIII

THE COMING OF THE SAVIOR: THE MAN-GOD

HUMANITY had long expected the Savior promised to our first parents. From afar Noe had hailed Him in the posterity of Sem. Abraham had known that in Him all generations of the earth should be blessed; Jacob had seen Him shining "like a star" amongst his descendants. Afterwards these promises in the course of the ages being multiplied and specified distinctly by the mouth of the Prophets of Israel and even of other nations, had, so to speak, written in advance the whole history of Him Who was to come and Who was called the Messias or Christ.[1]

The Christ was to be a son of David, but He should not appear until the scepter had departed from Judea; He would have an immediate Precursor who should announce His coming; the little town of Bethlehem had been designated as

---

[1] The word Messias comes from the Hebrew *Meschiah* which signifies "anointed or consecrated with holy oil" as king, Priest and Prophet. The Greek word *Christos* or Christ has the same meaning.

the place of His birth; He would restore the Kingdom of Israel, and His power should extend over the whole world; He would be the greatest of the Prophets; He would work numerous miracles; He would promulgate a new law; He would preach religion and would convert the nations to the worship of the true God, of the God of Abraham, of Isaac and of Jacob. And, on the other hand, texts strangely precise announced the humiliations, the sufferings and the death of this universal King of whose Kingdom there should be no end. He would give up His life as a sacrifice; He would bear the weight of our sins; He would intercede for the guilty. On this occasion the destruction of the city and of the Temple of Jerusalem was also predicted; the sacrifices were to cease; desolation should reign over the people, and a new Alliance should be inaugurated between God and man.

How were all these different predictions to be reconciled? Some 750 years had now elapsed since the foundation of Rome. The last king of Judea, Sedecias, taken to Babylon, had long since died there, and Judea now a province of the Roman Empire was governed by Herod, a native of Idumea. Nearly the whole of Europe, Northern Africa and a part of Asia were united under the dominion of Cæsar Augustus. The wars of conquest were at an end; peace reigned everywhere, and the world was resting in a state of mysterious expectation.

Now, on a day which has since been fixed as the 25th March and named the Feast of the Annunciation, an angel, the Angel Gabriel, appeared to a holy maiden of Nazareth in the country of Judea. She was called Mary and was the daughter of Joachim and Anne, and had just been espoused to a man named Joseph, both belonged to the ancient family of David, King of Juda.

And the Angel said to the Virgin —

"Hail, full of grace, the Lord is with thee: blessed art thou among women."

And he added

"Behold thou shalt conceive in thy womb, and shalt bring forth a son; and thou shalt call his name Jesus.[1]

He shall be great, and shall be called the Son of the most High; and the Lord God shall give unto him the throne of David his father; and he shall reign in the house of Jacob forever.

And of his kingdom there shall be no end."

Mary, troubled, and disquieted, said to the Angel —

"How shall this be done, because I know not man?"

And the Angel answered:

[1] The word, *Jesus*, in Hebrew, *Jeshua*, signifies *Savior*.

"The Holy Ghost shall come upon thee, and the power of the most High shall overshadow thee. And therefore also the Holy which shall be born of thee shall be called the Son of God."

Nine months afterwards in the little village of Bethlehem whither Mary had gone with Joseph, in a humble grotto in which the shepherds of the neighborhood sometimes found shelter, the Child came into the world at midnight of the twenty-fifth of December.

At that moment the Angels crowd round the stable in which the Infant lies, the neighboring shepherds hasten to pay Him homage, and later guided by a marvelous light, the Eastern Magi[1] in their turn arrive to acknowledge Him, and to offer Him their gifts in the name of the whole human race.

Eight days after His birth the Child was circumcised according to the Jewish custom, and received the name of Jesus. And as Herod, the King of Jerusalem, sought Him that he might put Him to death, Joseph and Mary, warned by an Angel, carried Him away into Egypt. Then Herod being dead, the Holy Family returned to Nazareth, where Jesus remained until He was thirty years of age, unknown, obedient, and spending His days in toil. When He had reached the

[1] The name given to the three Kings who came from the East to adore the Infant God.

age of thirty, Jesus left Nazareth and began to
manifest Himself to the world by going to find
John the Baptist who was preaching penance on
the banks of the Jordan and pouring water on
the heads of his disciples in signification of the
remission of their sins, whilst he announced the
approaching appearance of the Messias. Jesus
also was baptized, and whilst He prayed, Heaven
opened and the Holy Ghost appeared over Him
in the form of a dove, and from on high a Voice
was heard saying: "This is My beloved Son in
Whom I am well pleased." And John declared
"Behold him who taketh away the sins of the
world."

The mission of the Savior had commenced.
He chose twelve men, the twelve Apostles,[1] of
whom Peter was made head. With these He
journeyed through town and country, everywhere
hailed as the Messias or Christ and proclaimed the
Son of God, with a word healing the sick, raising
the dead to life, working miracles with the facility
and simplicity of a master who commands all
Nature; humble, meek, compassionate towards
the lowly, the poor, and sinners, firm when
necessary, always just, attracting to Himself
wonder-stricken crowds, and announcing under
the name of the Kingdom of God or the Kingdom
of the Heavenly Father the new society which

---

[1] *Apostle* from the Greek, Ἀπόστολος, messenger.

He came to establish on earth, and which, later, was to people Heaven. And the people said: "Never man spoke like this man:" because this man, indeed, was a Man-God.

"Now," says the Evangelist, "all this was done that it might be fulfilled which the Lord spoke by the prophet, saying:

Behold a virgin shall be with child, and bring forth a son, and they shall call his name Emmanuel, which being interpreted is, *God with us.*" (St. Matth. I. 22, 23.)

Such is the Mystery of the Incarnation or "of the Word of God made flesh," according to the sublime expression of the Apostle, St. John: two natures, the divine nature and human nature subsisting in the one sole Person of Jesus, the Messias, the Man-God.

He is Man, that is to say, He has a body like unto our body, formed from the Blood of His most holy Mother, and hence He is the Son of Adam and our Brother; this body is animated by a soul created for Him, a human soul endowed with the same natural faculties as our soul, sensible, intelligent, free. For this reason Jesus was born weak, unable to speak; He grew; He labored; He was humble and obedient; He prayed; He rejoiced at the happiness of His own; He was troubled; He wept; He loved His family, His disciples, His country; He has known pity, sadness, physical and mental suffering, everything "save sin" says St. Paul.

But this humanity of Christ is united to God inseparably in one and the same person; so that all the thoughts and all the actions of Jesus Christ are, in truth, divine thoughts and actions; all His merits are infinite; He is, at once, the Son of Man and the Son of God. He is the incarnate Word.

Therefore His Flesh, His Blood, His Heart — in which moreover, we see the symbol of His infinite love for us — are worthy of all our adoration. And for this reason also we give, and justly, to the Virgin Mary, His Mother, the title of "Mother of God;" not, assuredly, because she is the Mother of the divine Nature, but because she is the Mother of a Child who is God. And it is because of this unique quality that she herself, was born "immaculate" that is to say "free from original sin" or (what comes to the same thing), raised from the instant of her conception to the supernatural state of grace.

No comparison, evidently, can make us understand this great mystery of the Incarnation of the Son of God, the second Person of the Blessed Trinity. However let us suppose a crystal vase taken out of darkness and exposed to the sun; is it not as it were transformed by the sun, which penetrates it without taking from it any of its properties, or without the sun itself losing anything of its splendor? Thus is it with the Person of the Man-God. The human nature of Christ, penetrated by the rays of that divine Sun which is the Eternal Word, is transformed without the latter losing anything of Its splendor.

The mystery of the Incarnation surpasses all human conception. But how admirable it is, how manifestly divine! Across the abyss which separates humanity from God a bridge was necessary; none could make this bridge save God Himself; He has made it. And the elements united in the Person of Christ, have been taken from the two extreme points which are to be reconciled; Earth and Heaven; Time and Eternity, the Finite and the Infinite; Man and God.

Once opened, the "Way" shall not be closed. Protestant doctrine represents to us a God coming to redeem the world, leaving it a book as guide, and this done, retiring into Eternity. How different is Catholic Truth! According to the Church's teaching, Christ the Incarnate Word continues to dwell amongst us; He lives with us; He is accessible to the lowliest, the most unhappy, the most indigent. By the Sacraments He distributes to those who desire it supernatural life; He speaks by the mouth of His Vicar; He maintains the relations of earth with heaven, and of heaven with earth. And at the same time that

He restores the divine plan of the Creation, He responds to the deepest needs of humanity; He aids it to rise to a loving union with His father: He is indeed "the Way, the Truth, and the Life." (St. John, XIV. 6.)

CHAPTER IX

OUR DIVINE SAVIOR SUFFERS AND DIES FOR MEN

AT that epoch the Jews, as we have said, were under the domination of the Romans.[1] Now, if many followed Jesus Christ as the Messias, many others sought His destruction. Jesus knew this. The Prophets had predicted in detail His Passion, and He Himself on several occasions had predicted that He would be betrayed, seized, condemned, and put to death, but that on the third day He would rise again.

Seeing, therefore, that the time had arrived, Jesus went to Jerusalem for the Pasch, which was the great festival of the Jews. There the people received Him enthusiastically; their favor but increased the jealousy of His enemies, and these determined to put Him to death.

The following Thursday our Lord celebrated

[1] The Roman Senate had named Herod the Great, who died in the year 4, King of Judea. His son, Antipas, became Governor of Galilee during the time that Pontius Pilate governed Judea; the two repaired to Jerusalem for the Pasch.

the Paschal Feast with His Apostles. On the Feast of the Pasch the Jews killed a lamb which was offered to God in sacrifice, and which was afterwards eaten: a figure of our divine Savior Himself, who, as a lamb, was to be immolated, and afterwards would be given to Christians in Holy Communion. This repast has been called the Paschal Supper or the Last Supper.

When it was ended, our Lord went to pray in the Garden of Gethsemane, and beholding the death which was about to befall Him, the sins of men, their ingratitude, their blasphemies, He fell into an agony and His Body was covered with a sweat of blood. During this time one of His Apostles, Judas, agreed for thirty pieces of silver to deliver Him into the hands of His enemies. Led by the traitor, the soldiers came to apprehend Jesus Whom they bound; they spat upon His sacred Face, and then put Him in prison. The following day, Friday, our Lord was brought before His judges, and having declared that He was the Messias and the Son of God, the Jewish multitude, now turned against Him, cried out to Pilate "Away with him; crucify him." And as Pilate hesitated, saying, as he washed his hands before the people, "I am innocent of the blood of this just man," they answered, "His blood be upon us and upon our children." And so it happened; the Jews, perpetrators of the greatest crime ever committed on earth, the slaying of the Man-God, have been dispersed all over the earth and abandoned to their blindness.

Condemned to death, our Lord was taken away and struck in the face; in derision they put on His sacred head a crown of thorns; they scourged Him with leather thongs; then laying upon Him a heavy cross they led Him to an adjacent hill, Calvary, where He was crucified between two thieves. It was noonday. About three o'clock, Jesus seeing that His mission was accomplished, cried out "It is consummated." And soon afterwards saying: "Father, into Thy hands I commend My spirit," He expired, being then about thirty-three years of age.

Suddenly the earth trembled; the rocks were rent asunder; the sun was obscured; the end of the world seemed to have come. The terrified Jews dispersed, saying to one another: "What have we done? truly this was the Son of God."

Finally a soldier approached to see if Jesus were dead, and he pierced His side with a lance. Then the Sacred Body was taken down from the Cross, and laid in a tomb hewn in a rock, and a guard was placed over it.

Thus passed Friday evening and Saturday until Sunday morning. This voluntary death of Jesus Christ, the Son of God made Man, who expired on a Cross for the salvation of the world, completes the mystery of the Redemption, that is to say, of the deliverance of mankind from the thraldom of sin and of the demon.

Hence the Church in the Creed drawn up by the Councils of Nice (A.D. 325) and Constantinople (A.D. 381), thus acclaims Jesus Christ "Who for us and for our salvation, came down from heaven, and became incarnate by the Holy Ghost of the Virgin Mary; and *was made Man.* He was crucified also for us, suffered under Pontius Pilate, and was buried."

"Consummatum est." What do these words mean? Adam, who represented in himself the human race had been created in a supernatural state, and also was endowed both in his soul and body with extraordinary privileges. Original sin in one instant caused him to lose all both for himself and his descendants.

What would God do?

Urged by a love of which we can form but a very poor idea, He has deigned in the Person of His Son to take upon Himself our human nature, as a new Adam to supersede the first, to make reparation for Sin, and to merit the reintegration of the human race in the supernatural Order — which permits of union with God on earth by grace, and in Heaven by glory.

Such is the Redemption. The whole Christian Religion, says St. Augustine, can be summed up in the parts played by two men: the one who ruined us; the other who has saved us.

The Redemption is universal, in this sense, that it is extended to all men, for all sins, and for all the supernatural goods lost by our first father. But the extraordinary prerogative which the first man enjoyed with regard to concupiscence, the miseries of this life, suffering and death, have not been restored to his descendants; only to the elect in Heaven will these be given again.

Further, conformably to the original plan of the Creation, man retains freedom with regard to his actions; he is free therefore to profit or not to profit by the favor of this Redemption, free to remain dead in sin or to raise himself to the life of grace: with all the consequences which result from one or the other state for time and for eternity.

Thus, therefore, Jesus Christ has given to each of the sons of Adam the possibility of becoming supernatural, of being saved, through the merits of the Redemption. But it remains with them to apply these merits through the means which our divine Redeemer has given to us: these are faith, prayer, good works and the Sacraments; in these consist the *regeneration of man*.

The Lutheran doctrine asserts that Faith of itself alone suffices for the gaining of the merits of the Redemption; this is at once contrary to Holy Scripture, to justice, and to common sense.

The Redemption is, as it were, a decree of general amnesty granted by God through the intervention of our Lord. But to profit by it, we must first understand and accept it, and afterwards fulfil the requisite conditions.

And thus in its essential part God's design in the Creation of Man is restored.

CHAPTER X

RESURRECTION OF OUR LORD AND HIS ASCENSION
INTO HEAVEN

IN consequence of original sin Heaven was closed to Man. But from the beginning of the world countless numbers of the just had died: what had become of their souls? They were assembled in that mysterious abode called Hell or Limbo where they expected in peace the coming of the Messias, as on earth the living also expected Him. Our divine Lord being dead, His soul went to visit and to console these holy souls for whom had come at last the hour when they should receive their reward and should see God. Hence those words of the Creed "He descended into Hell." [1]

Meanwhile the morning of the third day had come.

Suddenly the earth trembled as if fearful of keeping any longer the sacred Body of our divine Savior; a shining Angel appeared at the tomb,

---

[1] The word *Hell* here signifies the "lower regions." (Latin, *inferi*.)

which burst open; the guardians, stricken with fear, fell on the ground; Jesus Christ had risen from the dead.

He first appeared to Mary Magdalen and the holy women who had believed in Him, to the two disciples on the road to Emmaus, to Peter and to the Apostles gathered together in the Cenacle,[1] and then to the Apostle, Thomas, who was absent at the time of His first appearance, and whom He made touch the wound caused by the lance in His sacred Side.

During forty days, our Lord remained amongst His own, appearing to them frequently, finishing His instructions to them, and promising to send to them the Holy Ghost to direct them in the organization of the Church. It was during this time that He appointed Peter to be the Head of the Church or Society of His disciples which He had just established; that He instituted the Sacraments and gave to the Apostles the power to remit sins; that He revealed the meaning of the Scriptures and the fulfilment in His own person of the prophecies and the figures relating to the Messias.

Finally, having assembled His followers on the Mount of Olives, near Jerusalem, He said to them —

[1] Cenacle (cœnaculum) dining-room, in which the last supper took place.

"All power is given to me in heaven and in earth. Going therefore, teach ye all nations; baptizing them in the name of the Father, and of the Son, and of the Holy Ghost; teaching them to observe all things whatsoever I have commanded you: and behold I am with you all days, even to the consummation of the world." (Matth. XXVIII. 18–20.)

And blessing them, He ascended into Heaven before them, surrounded by the great multitude of souls who from the beginning had been waiting for His triumph over death that they might enter into glory.

It is in Heaven that He reigns, at one and the same time God and Man, the Savior of the world, the Redeemer of the human race, "seated at the right-hand of God," that is to say, exalted over all, and giving to our poor human nature which He has assumed the first place in Heaven after the Most High.

In Heaven, St. Paul tells us, Jesus Christ is "always living to make intercession for us" (Hebr. 795). Our Lord Himself had already said this in the prayer: —

"And not for them only do I pray (the Apostles) but for them also who through their word shall believe in me; . . .

"Father, I will that where I am, they also whom thou has given me may be with me; that

they may see my glory which thou hast given me,"
(St. John XVIII. 24.)

Thus Jesus Christ is our Mediator, the necessary
intermediary between God and man, "the Way,
the Truth, and the Life," without whom there
is no salvation for human souls. If therefore we
pray to the Blessed Virgin, to the angels and to
the Saints, it is because we recognize in them help-
ful friends who can intercede for us with Jesus
Christ; but He alone is the Savior.

Immortal King of ages, Jesus Christ presides
over the development of His work of Redemption
which is the Kingdom of God in the world. Whilst
some hear Him, serve Him, and help Him, even
to the point of heroism, others ignore Him,
others forget Him, others fly from Him, betray
Him, blaspheme Him. And so pass the years
and the centuries. Each day death sends more
than 100,000 souls before Him; Jesus Christ
judges them, and He waits. . . . He awaits the
hour in which He will stop the onward movement of the world. Then He will reappear in
His infinite Majesty. And all men from Adam
to the last of his sons shall rise to hear the solemn
confirmation of the sentence which will determine
their lot forever. For Jesus Christ, who has
redeemed them, will judge the living and the
dead. (Ch. XI.)

CHAPTER XI

"TELL the vision to no man" said our divine Lord after His transfiguration, to His Apostles, "till the Son of Man is risen from the dead." (Matth. XVII, 9.)

Then it was, indeed, that Jesus Christ should be known and understood, when not only should He be accepted as the Messias or Christ, but when His Divinity should be revealed to the world.

Our Lord is chiefly known to us through the New Testament, and above all, through the four Gospels written by Saints Matthew, Mark, Luke and John, soon after our divine Savior's death. Considering them from an historical standpoint only, these are trustworthy accounts which before they were written, were either preached or related by eye-witnesses. The teaching thus given was called "the good tidings" and the name has remained in the writings in which it is contained.

Now in the Gospels, everything confirms those great words of St. Peter to Our Lord, "Thou art Christ the Son of the living God." (St. Matth.

82

XVI, 16.) In the first place, Jesus Christ clearly asserts His Divinity: "He is the Son of God" the Father and He "are but one." He is "the Word made flesh." And He demonstrates the truth of this assertion by a holiness of life, a power over nature, and a mass of proofs which could come from God alone.

For instance: in Him were fulfilled all the ancient prophecies concerning the Savior of the world. These prophecies follow one another in a continuous line throughout the ages, through the centuries; they are scattered throughout numerous texts of the Scriptures; it is impossible that they could be realized by chance, any more than by premeditation; they indicate the essential details of the Birth, the Life, the Death and the Resurrection of the Messias. Some of them assert His divinity. And in Jesus Christ all of them, one after another, are fulfilled.

Jesus Christ Himself declares that three days after His death He will rise again; that the Temple of Jerusalem shall be destroyed; that the Jews shall be dispersed over the world; that the Gospel shall be preached to all nations; that the Christian Religion shall endure to the end of the world in spite of all attacks and all persecutions. And all this has been verified before our eyes. With facility and calm ease before crowds of friends and enemies, He performs the most extraordinary miracles; with one word He allays the tempest; He multiplies the loaves and fishes; He cures the sick; He raises the dead to life. In other words, He commands nature as if He were its Author — as He is indeed — the elements, events, minds, consciences, sickness, death itself; He rules all, and He does so with a simplicity and a naturalness that do not belong to mere man.

His Apostles and His disciples also work miracles; but with this difference, they do so in the name of Jesus Christ, whilst Jesus Christ does so in His own name.

In His appearance, His character, His life, His teaching, His actions, He absolutely surpasses the greatest that have ever been seen amongst men. And yet none was ever more simple, more humble, meeker, none ever so indifferent to attitude, to eloquence, so devoid of self-seeking in any form whatever. It is God who hides Himself sufficiently to bring Himself within reach of man, and yet reveals Himself clearly enough to be recognized by those of good-will. "Never would the Jewish authors have conceived this manner or this mind; and in the Gospel there are characterics so truly great, so striking, so perfectly inimitable, that he who could invent them would be more astonishing than the hero." (J. J. Rousseau.)

In the same order of ideas Christianity is such

that it could only come from God. By its unity which connects it with the first beginnings of the world; its steadfastness in a doctrine which has developed without ever contradicting itself; its universality and adaptation to all nations, all countries, all times, all minds, the most backward equally with the most cultivated; by the coherence and the grandeur of its dogmas; the sublimity, the practical simplicity, and the social importance of its morality; in a word by all its characteristics, it evidently transcends all known religions. All that these have of good it possesses, and in what belongs to itself essentially and which it has from its original source, it manifestly surpasses them. It is quite conceivable that a man in response to the aspirations of the society from which he himself had sprung may have been able to organize religions such as Islamism, Brahmanism, Buddhism, etc. But dogmas such as those of the Trinity, of the supernatural order, of the Fall, of the Incarnation, of the Redemption, of the transmission of grace, etc. these could not enter into the conceptions of the human mind, above all with the unity and coherence which these dogmas present in Christianity.

Finally it is very remarkable that of all religions, the Christian Religion alone, in spite of persecution, of opposition, and of obstacles of every kind, has developed and spread over the whole earth;

the Christian Religion alone has ever triumphantly answered all the objections made to it; the Christian Religion alone proclaims itself the infallible guardian of the Truth, and alone proclaims as its immediate Author a God.

Let us return to Jesus Christ. When He judges that the term of His mission has come, He permits Himself to be seized and to be nailed to a Cross. His death is verified by the piercing of His sacred side with a lance, and He is buried in a tomb hewn in a rock which is guarded by soldiers. On the third day, as He had said, He appears once more living. During forty days He shows himself to His Apostles, to His disciples, to His friends, to His enemies, and He ascends into Heaven in the presence of a crowd which He has assembled and to whom He leaves His testament. After Him, all His Apostles and disciples assert His divinity; thousands of martyrs prefer to die rather than to deny Him; millions upon millions of souls—the best, the purest, the most beautiful—during twenty centuries have everywhere followed Him; served Him; adored Him, prepared for His sake to suffer everything.

And He, Jesus Christ, reveals Himself to these souls with a clearness, a force, a sweetness, which no intellectual proofs can replace. But if we would thus perceive Him, we must belong to Him wholly.

God alone can furnish so many witnesses. Hence if in this question of the divinity of Christ we are deceived, in truth it is God Himself Who deceives us. And as God Who is infinite Truth, Justice and Holiness could not have deceived men, — the most intelligent, the most devoted, the best of men for twenty centuries, we conclude by repeating with a faith that henceforth nothing can shake. *Jesus, Thou art my Savior and my God!*

Thus Jesus Christ in Person appears to us now in full light. Man and God in one sole individuality, He is in Creation as a central point to which everything tends, from which everything originates, around which everything revolves. He joins the world to the supernatural Order, He raises the sons of Adam after they have fallen, and brings Heaven within the reach of Humanity.

He is our Model, the Model of all virtues. Under the most diverse conditions, in the most opposite situations, He alone of all men, has said and can ever say to each one of them: *"Imitate Me."* And it is, in reality by trying to imitate Him that man by degrees raises himself to the perfection of the moral life.

He is our Doctor, our Prophet and our Master, having come to recall to mind the teachings of the primitive Religion, to state them clearly, to extend them, to complete them, so that no one henceforth should have authority to add to them one iota. He alone has given us clear and definite ideas of the meaning of the Creation, on the end of life, on God, on the human soul, on the present and the future life. He is our Savior, Savior at once by His doctrine, His example, His actions, His sufferings, and above all by His death which crowns the Work of our Redemption. By this also He is our Priest, offering Himself in a sacrifice of infinite value to acknowledge God's supreme dominion over the world, to return Him thanks, to obtain our pardon, and to beg of Him to continue His benefits. He is indeed the Lamb offered as a holocaust upon the Altar of Calvary Who taketh away the sins of the world, and Who reconciles men with their Creator.

Having become our Mediator on earth, He remains in Heaven our Mediator with His Father. In Heaven He is our Head, our Guide, our Lord, and according as death liberates human souls, He decides their lot whilst waiting until the end of time when He will appear as the universal Judge of *the Living and the Dead*.

Assuredly our intellect will never understand how the Word of God, God Himself, has been united to human nature in such a manner as to become as one of us in all things with the exception of concupiscence and sin. But what are we that we should analyze these mysteries and fathom these depths? Let us bow down before the facts, before the Truth, and adore.

"In the beginning," writes St. John, in the prologue to his Gospel — "was the Word, and the Word was with God, and the Word was God. The same was in the beginning with God. All things were made by him: and without him was made nothing that was made. In him was life, and the life was the light of men: And the light shineth in darkness, and the darkness did not comprehend it. There was a man sent from God, whose name was John. This man came for a witness, to give testimony of the light, that all men might believe through him. He was not the light, but was to give testimony of the light. That was the true light, which enlighteneth every man that cometh into this world. He was in the world, and the world was made by him, and the world knew him not. He came unto his own, and his own received him not. But as many as received him, he gave them power to be made the sons of God, to them that believe in his name. Who are born, not of blood, nor of the will of the flesh, nor of the will of man, but of God. And the Word was made flesh, and dwelt among us (and we saw his glory, the glory as it were of the only-begotten of the Father) full of grace and truth." (Ch. XII.)

CHAPTER XII

THE HOLY GHOST

The Supernatural Life — Grace

BEFORE ascending into Heaven Jesus Christ had promised His Apostles to send to them the Holy Ghost who would give them light and strength to preach the Gospel to Jerusalem, throughout Judea, and to the ends of the earth.[1]

Now ten days after the Ascension, on the Feast of Pentecost whilst they were assembled in the Cenacle, behold, suddenly there was a great noise as of the wind blowing with violence. And they saw what appeared like tongues of fire which, dividing, rested upon each one of them. Immediately *they were filled with the Holy Ghost;* and they understood all that had been taught to them previously.[2] They felt strong enough to pro-

[1] *Spirit* from *spiritus*, a breath. The Holy Spirit is as the breath of love proceeding from the Father and the Son.

[2] *Pentecost* (in Greek meaning *fiftieth*). A feast which the Jews celebrated fifty days after the Pasch, to recall the promulgation of the Law given to Moses on Mount Sinai.

claim the Gospel everywhere and they set out:
the Catholic Church was founded, the complete
and definite expansion of the primitive and of the
Mosaic Religion.

"What is now called the Christian Religion"
writes St. Augustine, "existed amongst the ancients, and from the beginning of the human race
has never ceased to exist, until Christ Himself
being come in the flesh, the true Religion which
existed before, began to be called Christian."
(Retract., 1, 13.)

Thus God works through the three Persons of
His mysterious Trinity to establish His Kingdom
in the world.

These three divine Persons are inseparable, and
one cannot act without the other. But each one
by special manifestation has revealed Himself.
And thus it is that the work of Creation and the
general providence of the salvation of Man have
been attributed to the special action of the eternal
Father. The Son by becoming Incarnate in human nature and in acquiring by His life, His sufferings, and His death an infinite treasure of merit
with His Father, accomplishes this Redemption.
Finally the divine Spirit by inspiring the Prophets
and the Sacred Writers, prepares this coming of
the Savior. He gives to the Eternal Word,
about to become incarnate, the most perfect
Mother that could be found amongst the daugh-

ters of Eve, and the Redemption being accomplished, through the ministry of the Church and through Himself, He pours out the benefits of it on every soul "of good-will."

In this last mission His action is twofold: In a general way the Divine Spirit directs and vivifies the Society established by Jesus Christ to spread the teaching of religious Truth and to distribute the fruits of the Redemption. He is, as it were, the soul of the Church, and it is in this quality that on the day of Pentecost He took possession of it under the visible form of tongues of fire.

But He is also the source of man's spiritual regeneration. From the state of spiritual death in which our souls were, He causes them by the grace of Baptism (or an equivalent grace) to be born again in the supernatural order; afterwards, He enlightens them; He fortifies them; He assists them. And it is this taking possession by the Divine Spirit of human souls throughout the entire universe which constitutes that interior Kingdom of God announced by the Prophets, which was so little understood by the Jews, which as each new soul is conquered, ever advances a little further, but which will have its full expansion only in Heaven beneath the gaze of the "Immortal King of Ages." This is why this invisible Kingdom cannot be assailed by attacks from outside;

it extends beyond all the frontiers, and it survives all the attempts of the enemy.[1]

This operation of God or of the Holy Ghost in the soul of man may be either habitual or transient. When *habitual* it is called *sanctifying grace;* "sanctifying," because it renders the soul holy, just, pure, a friend of God, adopted by Him as a child is adopted by its father, and His heir with Christ in all that concerns the ineffable goods of the Heavenly Kingdom. In sanctifying grace is comprised a twofold element; the dwelling of the Blessed Trinity or of the Holy Ghost in the human soul, and as a result, a supernatural quality which makes it a participator in the divine Nature. By this quality the soul is made divine. "As light," says St. Thomas, "proceeds from the presence of the sun, so grace results from the presence of the Divinity in Man." Because God lives in the just man, not only in that general manner in which He is everywhere present, but in a particular way as Father and Friend. And this union is progressive; it becomes more intimate according as the soul enriches itself by the practise of the Christian virtues, as is seen in the life of the Saints. But it can also disappear with grace, as the light disappears in the lamp in which it

[1] It is this interior Kingdom of God which constitutes what is called *the Soul of the Church.*

was shining; and the result of mortal sin is to cause its disappearance.

In this state of sanctifying or habitual grace the acts of virtue performed by man are *meritorious*, that is to say, being morally united to the merits of Our divine Savior, they constitute a right to spiritual favors and to the rewards of the future life. But the action of the Holy Ghost within us can also be transient. It is then "actual grace" which is characterized by acts more or less frequent, more or less prolonged, and consists in special helps which enlighten our mind and assist our will — a good thought, a good desire, a good impulse, — without however depriving us of our free will.

God, Who wills the salvation of all men, knows how to bring within the reach of every one the necessary aids. Infidels of good faith, for instance, are not excluded from this call. "We know" wrote Pius IX, "that those who through invincible ignorance are ignorant of our holy Religion, but who observe the natural law and are disposed to follow the precepts which God has inscribed on the conscience of all, are leading a just and upright life and can with the help of divine light and of grace acquire eternal life." (Pius IX, Encyclical. of 10. Aug., 1863.)

Thus the Holy Spirit fills the universe, and everywhere in it maintains the *supernatural life* which is otherwise called the *Christian Life*.

May this life be always ours!

Devotion to the Holy Spirit, the Inspiration of all light, of all energy, of all consolation, of all life, of all supernatural love, is at once very elevated and very simple. It uplifts us at once above earthly miseries; inspires us with the most exalted and the most delicate sentiments, and is for us in the obscurity which enshrouds our path as a luminous and beneficent cloud which guides our steps.

Let us think of the Holy Ghost; let us live in Him, invoke Him. Who is there that does not need to be enlightened, to be fortified, to be consoled. In Him we shall find light, strength, and consolation.

Hence true Christians practise the excellent devotion of praying to the Holy Ghost every morning before beginning the labor of the day, whenever they have some important decision to make, and in all the difficult circumstances, sorrows, trials, doubts and troubles of life.

CHAPTER XIII

The Only Rule of Our Faith

JESUS Christ is God. Having come on earth to establish in souls His spiritual Kingdom and to prepare the way for them to Heaven, He might have remained here visible and accessible to all. But thus to multiply miracles is not in the order of Providence. He could have left a precise code of His teaching and of His Law established once and for all, in which each one might have sought personal direction. But this is a purely human conception which in Religion would have occasioned the most varied interpretations, and ended in deplorable confusion. He has done better: He has confided the deposit of His doctrine and the organization of Religion to an Authority, human, living, compassionate towards our weakness, accessible to the humblest, conforming to the reasonable requirements of the times and of the nations, an Authority with whom He has promised to remain, in order to assist her, until the end of time.

To this Authority Jesus Christ Himself has given a name: the Church. (St. Matthew, XVIII, 17.)

The word comes from the Greek *ecclesia* (from *eccalein*, to call, to convoke) which signifies at once *meeting* and place of *meeting* that is, in this last sense, the local or parish Church. In a wider sense it is also the society of the Faithful of some particular region: the Church in Jerusalem, the Church in Paris, in America, in France, etc. Finally, in its widest acceptation it is *"the Society of all the Faithful* who profess the same Christian Faith, participate in the same Sacraments and are governed by lawful pastors under the Authority of the same Roman Pontiff." (Bellarmine.) This Universal Society, by an uninterrupted course of beliefs, of moral laws, and of religious observances, is connected with the first man and will end only with the last.

In the beginning the Church was composed of Jesus Christ, of His Apostles, His disciples: and all those who believed in Him. His teachings completed without contradicting those of the Ancient Tradition and of the sacred Books: He was the link between the Old and the New Testament.

When His earthly mission was drawing to a close, Jesus Christ chose a substitute, a *Vicar* who after Him was His visible representative, authorized and furnished with the necessary powers and prerogatives to continue His great Work and to direct souls to eternal salvation.

This first Head of the Catholic Church was the Apostle Simon, surnamed Peter. "Thou art Peter," said Our Lord to him, "and upon this rock I will build My Church and the gates of hell shall not prevail against it." (St. Matth., XVI, 18.)

To this Head He promised assistance that he might never be deceived or deceive us in the teaching of Religion. "Simon, Simon, — I have prayed for thee, that thy faith fail not." (St. Luke, XXII, 32.)

To him also He entrusted supreme power to establish in souls supernatural life. "I will give unto thee the keys of the kingdom of heaven: and whatsoever thou shalt bind on earth shall be bound in heaven; and whatsoever thou shalt loose on earth shall be loosed in heaven." (St. Matth., XVI.)

Finally, comparing the multitude of the Faithful to a docile flock which must remain united under the Shepherd's care, Jesus Christ, said to Peter: "Feed my lambs," (that is to say: the Faithful); "feed my sheep" (the Bishops and Priests). (St. John, XVI.)

Thus appointed chief of the Apostles, Peter in the beginning went to live in Antioch, where the first of the Faithful took the name of Christians, that is to say, disciples of Christ. Then he passed to Rome, at that time the capital of the civilized world, and there, in the year 67, he was martyred. There also from that time until now his successors to the number of 265, have resided.

They are called Popes, from a Greek word signifying father, the Pope being in truth the father of the whole Christian family, and because of the place of his central administration the *Catholic Church* is also the *Roman Church*.

As the Church developed as every society develops, she has always retained her fundamental organization. Under the authority of the supreme Pastor, the successor and representative of Christ, she advances towards Heaven like a flock sure of the road, Pastors and Faithful ever closely united, one with the other.

Under the direction of the Pope the Pastors are the Bishops and Priests who are charged with the instruction in the truths of Religion of the assemblies of the Faithful entrusted to them, with the duty of distributing to them supernatural life or grace by means of the Sacraments, and of governing them in the religious department of their life. For this reason at their ordination and consecration they receive a special character and special powers.[1]

[1] The Bishop (in Greek, ἐπίσκοπος, he who superintends) has the spiritual administration of a certain region called a *diocese*. The

All the other members of the Church form the Faithful. They exercise no sacred ministry, but as far as circumstances permit, they should lend their aid to the pastors in doing good to those around them, in safeguarding the Faith in souls and in contributing to the propagation of the Kingdom of God on Earth.

Thus the *Hierarchy of the Church* is organized in such a manner that the faithful are subordinate to their priests, the priests to their Bishops, and the Bishops to the Pope, the supreme Pastor of Christ's flock.[1]

Those who of themselves or under the influence of false shepherds refuse to follow this supreme Pastor who "has the words of eternal life," who rebel against him and form a band apart, are warned, then they are judged, and finally they are cut off from the whole of the flock: these are the excommunicated, the schismatics, and the heretics.[2] Having been baptized, they are Christians, but they are no longer Catholics and they can only be restored to the Church by making their

---

word Priest comes from the Greek $\pi\rho\epsilon\sigma\beta\acute{v}\tau\epsilon\rho\sigma$, ancient (the first priests having been chosen from amongst the elders). The Faithful are those who have the Faith and who live in conformity to it.

[1] *Hierarchy*, that is to say, order and organization which subordinates inferiors to superiors.

[2] *Excommunicated*, that is to say, cut off from the communion or community; *schismatic*, one separated by schism; heretic, one attached to a heresy (condemned doctrine).

submission to the Sovereign Pontiff and by returning to the common way followed by all the Faithful.

In order to settle these disputes, to make laws suited to the times, to condemn current errors, to declare that such or such a truth forms part of the deposit of the Faith, the Pope at times assembles the Bishops in meetings which are called Councils. Such was the Council of Trent (XVI century) in which the Protestant heresy was condemned and the unity of the Church was preserved; such also was the Vatican Council (1869–1870) in which the infallibility of the Pope in all matters of Faith was proclaimed.

From what we have said, the Church from the beginning appears to us as being the depository of the teachings of Jesus Christ. From Him she received all power to organize and govern herself with a command to proclaim the Gospel to all human beings.

These teachings of which the Church has been constituted guardian were quickly set forth in writing under the impulse and guidance of divine inspiration; and hence we have the Gospels, the Acts of the Apostles, the Letters or Epistles, the Apocalypse, in other words, the New Testament, which is the continuation and the completion of the Old.

Historically, therefore, the Church is presented

to us as the only living Rule of our Faith. And this simple statement destroys the very foundations of Protestantism and of all the heresies which claim to be grounded on the pure Gospel. But it is from the Church that we have received the pure Gospel, and, having given it to us, she alone has authority to explain the meaning.

"There were no heretics in existence yesterday," says St. Augustine, "and they would not have had the Gospel if they had not stolen it when they fled from the Father's house." (St. Augustine, *Epist. contra Manich*, 1, 1.)

Hence, having demonstrated her divine origin, the mission which she has received, and the assistance promised to her, the Church presents herself to the world bearing in her hands the Deposit of the Faith, constituted of Scripture and Tradition. And from this she draws with all necessary authority the teachings which she believes herself bound to give the Faithful for the guidance of their lives and the salvation of their souls.

Therefore it is not from the Scriptures alone that we prove the divine origin of the Church. The Church herself first proves her divine origin and then presents to us the Scriptures with all the marks of authenticity and of veracity to be desired.

In the beginning, until about the year 42,

Christian Society and the Catholic Church were one, and possessed none of the New Testament in writing: all the teaching of the Church was oral or from tradition. None the less was she the undisputed Guardian of Belief, of Morality and of Worship.

What the Church was then, she has remained.

In other words, we begin by applying the ordinary rules of scientific inquiry to prove the authenticity and the veracity of the books of the New Testament. These books regarded afterwards as historical prove the fact of the institution of the Church by Christ; and the Church thus proved to be a divine fact, can in its turn lawfully demonstrate the divine origin of the Scriptures. Here we have no vicious circle, such as sometimes we have been reproached with; the reproach is unjust.

CHAPTER XIV

THE DISTINCTIVE MARKS OF THE CHURCH

IN order to distinguish the true Church from the false sects which should spring up beside her, as He had foreseen and predicted, Jesus Christ gave to her certain characteristics, marks or signs by which an unprejudiced mind could always recognize her.

In the first place, it is evident that Christ for the continuation of His mission on earth willed to establish not a vague association the members of which would be united only by interior aspirations, but a *real and visible Society* having its Head, its representatives, its doctrinal system, its code of morality, its worship, its Sacraments; in other words, a Society which should be also an Authority.

From the earliest ages the visible Society thus constituted, in its essential elements with Simon Peter as Head, with the Apostles, with the "Ancients" or "Priests" and with the disciples converted from Judaism or infidelity to whom was given very quickly the name of Christians, has performed its divinely appointed functions. In it the Apostles exercised the powers which they held from Jesus Christ; they preached; they taught; they judged; they remitted sins and administered the Sacraments; they organized the Faithful into small bodies which gradually grew larger. As these powers were to be exercised "until the end of time" and "amongst all mankind" they were naturally transmitted to the successors appointed by the Apostles, that is to say, to Bishops under the supreme authority of Peter and of Peter's successors.

On Peter, indeed Jesus Christ conferred the primacy, the primacy of honor and of jurisdiction; he was "to bind and to loose," to feed "the lambs and the sheep;" "to open the kingdom of Heaven;" he was to be the rock on which is built "the Church." For our divine Savior does not say "the Churches" but "the Church." He could not, moreover, it is quite clear, found several Churches, all adverse one to the other. Therefore there is but one only. Now, as the one and only Church is destined to last until the end of the world, its *oneness* must necessarily be assured by the *unity of its government* and the *primacy of its Head*. This Church is the Holy Catholic Apostolic Roman Church.[1]

This Society undoubtedly is a living organism the continual evolution of which must follow the

[1] Name used by the Vatican Council.

guiding line marked out for it, with such adaptations as time and circumstances may demand. But the Church of Leo XIII, of Pius X, and of Benedict XV differs no more from that of Simon Peter than the man differs from the child, than the flower differs from the bud. It is, according to the words of Jesus Christ Himself, the small seed cast into the ground which shoots forth, increases, and becomes a great tree without ceasing to be the same in its organic unity.

Composed of men of free will who are consequently capable of every virtue as of every weakness, the Church in this respect resembles every human Society. We should not therefore be surprised to find in her, during her long history, inferior and even unworthy elements. But this fact only brings out more clearly the divine origin of the interior principle which animates her, maintains her, and causes her to develop in spite of every obstacle; we may be saddened but our Faith can never be shaken. This Faith must indeed have its roots in deeper depths than superficial and unstable elements. The weakness of the instruments to whom the progress of the Church has been confided serves rather to bring out more clearly her supernatural origin. If the Church were a human institution, long ago, either by their attacks or their favors or their errors, men would have destroyed her.

Nor can the charge of "superstition" brought against some of her children injure her; these "superstitions" are like wild plants in a richly cultivated garden; they were not sown by the divine Master, they are not cultivated by His representatives, they sprang up of themselves; they will die out, unless, becoming too intrusive, they are uprooted and cast into the fire.

But what well may seem inexplicable is the hatred with which the Catholic Church has ever been and will be forever pursued. That the various attacks of which she is the object should be thus maintained throughout the long course of the ages almost compels us to believe that they are directed by an enemy who is immortal, by one whom we call "the Enemy." No opinion, no philosophical system, no religion, has ever provoked the opposition, the hostility which the Church has always encountered. And this also is a sign, pointed out moreover by Christ, which marks her divine origin.

The Church having received from Jesus Christ the promise that He would be with her until the end of time, and having as her mission the custody and the interpretation of the Word of God, she must be, and she is, infallible[1] in her teaching, otherwise she could not be a sure guide for man;

[1] Infallible — does not err — (Latin *infallere*) is not to be confounded with *impeccable*.

she could not direct them in the way of Truth and righteousness. A fallible Church not knowing what to believe about the truths which she is charged to teach, liable to err, and to mislead its subjects, could not be a divine institution.

This infallibility has been promised to the Head of the Church, to Peter and to his successors whenever, acting as Vicars of Jesus Christ and assisted by the Holy Ghost, these define, explain, or specify the religious truths contained in the Deposit of Revealed Truth, namely in Tradition or in Holy Scripture.

The Pope, therefore, when he only expresses his personal opinions or when he treats of matters foreign to the Faith is no more infallible than he is impeccable.

As has been remarked before, Revelation ended with Jesus Christ and His Apostles; the Church is but its guardian and interpreter. Therefore if, through the course of the ages for reasons which she judged good, she has defined certain truths as revealed, she has never given them as new truths, but on the contrary, as truths contained explicitly or implicitly in Holy Scriptures, or in the Apostolic Traditions.

It is the same, in due proportion, with those devotions and practices which the Church ordains or authorizes; such must be grounded on Revelation (the Scriptures or Apostolic Tradition) judiciously interpreted. But, we repeat, the Church cannot be responsible for the abuses and the travesties which may be made of these, any more than for the erroneous interpretations which may be given of them.

Other distinctive signs or characteristics make known to us the true Church of Christ. Our divine Redeemer has willed that His Church should be *One*, not divided into divers opposing sects, each one inimical to the other: *Apostolic*, for it is to the Apostles and their lawful successors that He has confided His Church: *Holy*, and provided with every means of sanctification, for her sole end and aim is to lead souls to God: *Catholic*, or universal, for He has come for all.

Now the Church of Rome, of which the Pope is the Head, alone possesses these four characteristics. Let us compare this Church with the various dissenting Churches. Not only have the Churches no *Unity*, but it may be said that there are as many forms of Protestantism as there are Protestants. They have not *Holiness*, for they began by revolt against lawful authority. They have not *Catholicity*, for each one can count but a small number of adherents, and the most ancient only goes back to the 16th century. They are not of Apostolic origin, for, manifestly they began — some in Germany with the monk Luther, others in England with Henry VIII, others in France and Switzerland with Calvin, etc.

For the rest, here is how the Church as regards her origin stands compared with the most ancient and the most important of the dissenting Churches: —

Name	Place of Origin	Founder	Date of Foundation
Catholic Church	Jerusalem	Jesus Christ	33
Greek	Constantinople	Photius	IX Century
		Michael Cerularius	IX Century
Russian	Moscow	Czar Feodor	1588
	Petrograd	Peter the Great	1721
Lutheran	Germany	Luther	1524
Calvinist	Strasburg	Calvin	1534
Anglican	England	Henry VIII	1534
Methodist	England	John & Charles Wesley	1743

"There shall be one flock, and one shepherd," says Jesus Christ. Where could there be found a more manifest denial of this great saying than in the present division of Christian Society into divergent branches, one of which rejects what the other maintains?

"One flock, one shepherd." When shall our

divine Lord's Will be accomplished? Alas: we are indeed far from it; and yet no one has the right to be indifferent about religion, for the simple reason that God is not indifferent about it, nor can He be. And if He Himself has taken the trouble to show us the way we should follow in order to attain to Him, is it not offering Him the greatest of insults to remain insensible to His call?

Hence it has been justly said that outside the Church there is no salvation. This saying, however, should be understood in its exact meaning.

Besides the visible members of the *body* of the Catholic Church, there are men well-disposed and of good faith in heretical, schismatic, and infidel countries who may be said to belong to her *Soul;* such are known to God alone and no one has the right to put a limit to His mercy.

"We must hold for certain" wrote Pius IX, "that those who through no fault of theirs are ignorant of the true religion cannot, in the sight of the Lord, be held responsible for their condition. Now, who will pretend to fix the limits of this ignorance according to the nature and the variety of the people, of the countries, of the minds, and of so many other circumstances? When, released from the fetters of this body of ours, we shall see God as He is, we shall understand in what a close and magnificent union mercy and justice are bound. But the gifts of

divine grace shall never be wanting to those who
with sincere hearts desire to be regenerated by
this light and who ask for it."

The divinely-established unity of the Catholic
Church is the reason of what is sometimes called
her intolerance. She cannot, in fact, accept any
other constitution than that which she has received from Jesus Christ and the Apostles, whilst
the Protestant and schismatic churches are free—
with a freedom of which they have availed themselves—to legislate for themselves as they please.

The Catholic Church cannot adopt any other
doctrines than those which she finds in the re-
pository of the Faith confided to her (and which
moreover contains nothing contrary to any proved
philosophical or scientific truth.) For a Catholic
Truth is one, and error is manifold. For a
Protestant, on the contrary, Religious truths
depending on private interpretation of the Scriptures are as varied as minds and consciences.[1]

Nor can the Church modify her moral code.
All that is permitted to her, is, as has been said,
to adapt her secondary regulations of discipline
and of worship to the times, the countries, and
the circumstances. This she has always done

[1] The Protestant Church is in reality, only composed of persons
who "protest" — some against one point, the others against
another, of the doctrine accepted by the mass of the Christian
community.

and thence have originated, notably, those various rites, ceremonies, and observances of the Latin, Greek, Syriac, Coptic, Armenian, Arabic, Slav and other Churches which are all Catholic. This is variety in unity.

Happy are we if from childhood we have followed the Way of Truth, or if in the course of our life we have come to it, or if even now we are attaining to it. For once we admit that God is the Author and Ruler of the World; that Jesus Christ is the Man-God sent to teach men the end and aim of life, and the way to Heaven; that the Holy Catholic Apostolic Roman Church is the work of Jesus Christ — all becomes clear and simple. We have only to follow the Catholic Church in all that she teaches and prescribes to us, without being obliged every moment to ask ourselves: "Where is Truth?" By living and dying Catholics, we can live and die in peace. And this is the greatest of blessings.

CHAPTER XV

The Evangelizing of the World

FROM all that has been said, the end and aim of the Catholic Church, the reason of her existence and her mission in the world are sufficiently obvious.

The further we trace back towards our origin, the more we see that God has never abandoned Man. After having manifested to him religious Truth in its essential elements, Belief, Morality and Worship, with the Family to insure its guardianship and transmission, He chose for Himself a nation, the Jewish people, whom He made the special depository of His promises. Next, in the Person of Jesus Christ in whom are accomplished the prophecies and the figure of the Old Testament, He comes into direct touch with us. Afterwards, our divine Savior continues to live on earth by the institution of that visible Society which is the Catholic Church by means of which He reveals Himself to the whole world.

And thus all is harmonized; in spite of the bad use which too often man makes of his free will; in spite of our want of understanding, our opposition, our indifference, the divine Plan is unfolded before our eyes, bringing eternal salvation within the reach of souls of good-will.

Universal in her nature and in her end, the Catholic Church adapts herself to every form of government, but from all she requires, because she has the right to do so, liberty for her children; liberty to believe; liberty to teach; liberty to practise; liberty to form associations; liberty to organize; liberty to govern herself; liberty to possess the goods necessary to her; in a word, liberty to fulfil the supernatural mission entrusted to her by Jesus Christ. She can further demand that protection which is the right of a Society which propagates truth and virtue, and is the greatest factor in peace and order.

The Catholic Church has not as her direct end the development of wealth, of commerce, of industry, of well-being, nor the advancement of literature, of art, or science, but she is far from being uninterested in material, intellectual, and social progress; quite the contrary.

She is the best and most solid upholder of the Family, which is the essential basis of Society; she has exalted the dignity of womanhood; ennobled virginity; emancipated the slave; protected and helped childhood, the aged, the sick, the poor; all that are weak, all that are unhappy. To Paganism which gives all rights to force and cunning, she has opposed the law of mildness, of compassion, of love.

The morality which she teaches is based on justice which gives to each one his due, and on charity the necessary complement to justice. She it was who first proclaimed the equality of men before God. Her principles are the best safeguard of liberty, of health, of sobriety, of order, of economy, of prudence, of all the domestic and of all the social virtues; that is to say, of the people's welfare.

Finally, she imposes herself on conscience itself, and thus she remains the strongest factor in civilization.

It is in this sense that a modern writer, not liable to be suspected of partiality, speaking of Christianity says:

"To-day, after eighteen centuries, as formerly among the artisans of Galilee, it still operates and in the same manner—the manner of substituting love of others for love of self. For 400 millions of human beings it is still the means of spiritual life, the great indispensable pair of wings to raise man above himself, above his groveling life, his limited horizon, to guide him through patience, resignation, and hope to serenity; to transport him upwards even beyond temperance, purity, and goodness to devotedness and self-sacrifice. Always and everywhere, for eighteen hundred years, as soon as these wings grow weak or are broken, both public and private morals become corrupt.

"In Italy during the Renaissance, in England under the Restoration, in France under the Convention and the Directory, we have seen man become, as in the first century, pagan; from the same cause, he became again, as he was in the time of Augustus, hard and voluptuous, using others ill and himself also. Inhuman calculating selfishness had regained the ascendancy; cruelty and sensuality displayed themselves everywhere; Society became a den of thieves, an abyss of infamy. When one has seen from a near point of view this spectacle, one can estimate the value of Christianity in our modern Society, the prudence, the kindness, the humanity which it introduces therein, the noble manners, the sincerity, the justice which it maintains. Neither philosophical reasoning, nor artistic and literary refinement, nor even honor, feudal, military, or chivalric, no code, no administration, no government suffices to render this service in its stead. It alone can stop us in our fatal descent; can check the insensible sliding by which our race incessantly and with all its original momentum retrogrades towards the depths below; the old Gospel, under whatever form it shows itself at present, is to-day the best auxiliary of the social instinct." (H. Taine, Revue des Deux Mondes, 1891.)

But the particular mission of the Catholic Church is to continue the mission of Jesus Christ, the Savior of the world: to spread and develop in souls, all the souls to which it can reach, Religious Truth and Christian Life, having regard to the Kingdom of God on earth and in Heaven. Such was the last command and as it were the last Testament of our divine Redeemer. The hour of His return to His Heavenly Father having come, Jesus Christ assembled His Apostles and disciples who at that time formed the whole of the Church, on the Mount of Olives and said to them "All power is given to me in heaven and in earth. Going therefore teach ye all nations: baptizing them in the name of the Father, and of the Son, and of the Holy Ghost; teaching them to observe all things whatsoever I have commanded you: and behold I am with you all days, even to the consummation of the world." (St. Matth. XXVIII. 18.) And ascending into Heaven, Jesus vanished from sight. Such is the supreme testament left to the Church, not as advice or counsel, but as a solemn, clear, precise order.

Not only has the Church the right to execute

this order, but it is her duty. For this has she been founded. And as long as there remains on earth one single nation, one single family, one single man that has not received the divine message, she cannot be at rest, for the will of our divine Savior would not be fully carried out. For this reason the Church from the time of Saint Peter until now has always sent missionaries to the world; the human race is her audience.

Now, if from the point which we occupy on the globe, we turn our eyes to the distant horizon, what do we see? About 1,500 millions of human beings. Of these 250 to 300 millions belong to the visible Body of the Catholic Church. 200 to 250 millions are baptized Christians believing in Jesus Christ and expecting salvation from Him, but separated from the visible Body of the Church (schismatics, heretics, etc.). Eleven millions are Jews, 200 millions are Mussulmans, not baptized, but alike believing in a God who will reward the good and punish the wicked; they obey a moral law and believe in a future life. 680 millions are infidels, properly so called, without any precise faith, and amongst whom the remains of primitive Religion can scarcely be distinguished, buried as they are in a mass of absurd or cruel superstitions. All these men are our brethren, all these souls have been ransomed by the Blood of a God; nineteen centuries have passed, but, alas, they have not yet received the great tidings of salvation. And this is owing to the fact that the Church can only execute the divine Master's last Testament in as far as her children come to her assistance.

They can and they should so do, some by becoming missionaries, others by helping the Missions with their sympathy and financial aid according to their circumstances and opportunities; all should help by praying for the propagation of the Gospel.

In accordance with the all-ruling plan of Providence the evangelizing of the world is to a large degree subject to the general trend of human events. Our cooperation therefore must accommodate itself to what we can discern of God's designs, and become more active according as new ways open to us the far-off lands, as fresh means are afforded us of reaching the infidel nations, as new colonies create fresh obligations on us with regard to those races hitherto less favored, and for whom at last the day has come to live in the light of eternal Truth. Our age must be awake to its special duties.

In the beginning of the Christian era the Roman empire was at peace and extended almost over the whole of Europe to the North of Africa and a part of Asia; — a wonderful arrangement of Providence for the propagation of the Gospel. After the Roman empire had been evangelized, it was invaded by the "Barbarians" who in their turn received the glad tidings of salvation.

In the XVI century a New World was discovered whither immediately went the missionaries of God.

Finally, in our day before our eyes, the White Race, which in its entirety, it may be said, has been won to Christianity, has succeeded in subjecting to its dominion or its influence the nations which hitherto have eluded the operation of Jesus Christ.   But at the same time it has received the mission to bring to them Christian civilization.

This is the divine Master's order.   Let us go therefore; let us teach all nations and baptize them.

According to recent statistics the following figures will show the progressive stages of the Church's growth.

First Century		500,000	Catholics.
II.	"	2,000,000	"
III.	"	5,000,000	"
IV.	"	10,000,000	"
V.	"	15,000,000	"
VI.	"	20,000,000	"
VII.	"	25,000,000	"
VIII.	"	30,000,000	"
IX.	"	40,000,000	"
X.	"	56,000,000	"

Eleventh Century	70,000,000	Catholics.
XII. "	80,000,000	"
XIII. "	85,000,000	"
XIV. "	90,000,000	"
XV. "	100,000,000	"
XVI. "	125,000,000	"
XVII. "	185,000,000	"
XVIII. "	250,000,000	"
XIX. "	280,000,000	"

Hence the Catholic Church appears to us in the world like a long caravan in the midst of an immense desert. She advances, guided by her visible Head, the Vicar of Jesus Christ, sure of her road towards the eternal Oasis of Light and of Peace; the mysterious pillar of the cloud which guided Moses and the Hebrews to the Promised Land has been restored for her. Beyond and above all civil and political Societies, through all epochs, all climes, all civilization, speaking all tongues in her one and only catechism, recognizing as her own the children of every branch of the human family, white yellow, black, civilized and savage; often attacked, disregarded, criticized, betrayed, abandoned, she continues to advance, flinging to either side as she goes all those who have separated from her, Arius, Nestorius, Eutyches, Photius, Luther, Calvin, Rousseau, Voltaire and so many others. Many tremble as she passes; from afar many regard her with surprise or indifference, hatred or envy; many fight against her; many ignore her; some join her.

Still she advances.

O God, Who art "the Way, the Truth and the Life," if I am part of the great Caravan of the Catholic Church, grant that I may continue so until the end! And if I am not part of it grant that I may become so! For She alone "has the words of eternal Life."

CHAPTER XVI

THE COMMUNION OF SAINTS, THE FORGIVENESS
OF SINS

THAT God may be known, loved, and served in Heaven and on earth: such was and is the will of Jesus Christ; such is what the Catholic Church everywhere labors to obtain; such is what each one of us should of ourselves seek to attain, in ourselves first of all, and next in all those with whom we may come in touch. There is nothing material in this Kingdom of God.

When by His grace God is present in a soul, when that soul is pure and living, when she is not stained and as it were dead in consequence of sin, then God reigns in that soul.

Now, those living souls, adorned with God's grace and resplendent with the presence of the Holy Ghost, are found in three distinct Kingdoms. In Heaven where they receive the reward which they have merited and where they shall live forever: these form what we call the *Church Triumphant;* in Purgatory where after death, before entering Heaven, they complete their purification from every stain of sin, they are the *Church Suffering;* on earth where by battling against evil, they are trying to maintain themselves in good: these are the *Church Militant.*

But these three Societies in reality form but one, bound together as they are by one and the same supernatural life. They form one family, an immense family of which God is the Universal Father.

Hence we say to Him: "Our Father Who art in Heaven."

Jesus Christ Who calls Himself the "Son of Man" is, as it were, our eldest brother. He has brought us back to the Father. He has labored, suffered, and been afflicted for us, and He continues to help us on our journey to eternity. The Saints in Heaven are those of our brethren who have reached their final goal, and who can there be of use to us. They know us; they are interested in our salvation; they love us; they pray for us. So it is with the souls in Purgatory. And this beautiful union, this mutual help which we render one another, this participation in the same supernatural life, is what is called the Communion of Saints.

Let us imagine a large family at the head of which is the father, the master of all the property which is kept in reserve under his care. The eldest son, in an expedition in which he sacrificed his life to save his brothers, has acquired all that he wanted for himself, and in addition enough to ransom them from slavery, and to restore them to their paternal home. Amongst all the children of the family dispersed throughout the world, some have already returned to their father and have added their own wealth to the common treasury; others are on the road to him, profiting by the help which they render one another, and which they receive from their seniors; this is a figure of the Catholic Church united in the Communion of Saints.

God is the Father of the family; Jesus Christ is the eldest Son Who has ransomed us; the Blessed Virgin, the Apostles, the Martyrs and the Saints, our relatives who by a holy death have gone before us: these are our seniors who are in Heaven, and we are the rest of the family who are traveling to the eternal Father's Home.

As we journey, we are often mistaken; we go astray; we retrace our footsteps; we fall; we hurt ourselves, that is to say, we commit faults more or less numerous, more or less grave; and at times, alas! together with the grace of God we lose supernatural life. Nevertheless God does not abandon us. The Church by applying to us the merits of Jesus Christ and of the Saints, by means of the Sacraments can remit our sins, provided we repent of them; and thus pardoned we continue our journey, no doubt often falling, but rising up again, until one day we reach the end — a blessed eternity.

Marvelous unity of the Catholic Church, touching fraternity, admirable tenderness, which thus uplifts to God Himself the poorest and the humblest amongst men!

CHAPTER XVII

DEATH AND RESURRECTION

THIS life is short; what are 10, 20, 30, 50, even 80, even 100 years? But it is during these few years that each one of us must win or lose our happy eternity. If we win it, all is won; if we lose it, all is lost and forever.

Scarcely had Adam consummated his sin when God said to him: "Dust thou art, and unto dust thou shalt return." Since that day the children of Adam have multiplied and spread over the whole earth; where are they? Dust they were and into dust they have returned.

Like them, I, too, am a child of Adam, and, so like them, I too am condemned to die; every step that I take on the road of life brings me nearer to the grave into which I must descend. But where shall I die? When? And how? This is what I do not know. And because I know not, I must always be ready; I must always keep my soul pure and my conscience at rest.

What is death? Death is that which takes away the soul from the body, and leaves the body lying motionless, insensible, lifeless. The soul has gone and the body formed only of matter rapidly falls into decomposition. The Church, none the less, regards these mortal remains as sacred; they served as the temporary habitation of an immortal soul sanctified by grace; they shared in the merits of the human being; they were honored, perhaps, by contact with the Sacred Body and Blood of Jesus Christ. For these reasons the Church blesses these mortal remains and commits them to the earthly "*dormitory*" (which is the meaning of the word "cemetery") whilst she makes over them the sign of the Cross.

When this body, so soon to be reduced to dust, has been laid in the earth, the weeks, the months, the years, the centuries, shall pass, until with time itself all human generations shall have passed away, and the end shall have come. This end, when is it to be? No one knows. Our divine Redeemer tells us that "of that day or hour no man knoweth, neither the angels in heaven nor the Son, but the Father." (St. Mark XIII, 32) and we must abide by His words. This is a secret which God keeps. However in Holy Scripture some signs are given to us which may furnish us with some indications. The Gospel shall have been preached over the whole earth, after which, owing to the influence of seducers and of false prophets, a general weakening of faith will take place, resulting in the people being won away from the Church. "A 'man of sin' will appear, the 'Anti-Christ,' that is to say he who is 'against Christ,' who will have the power of Satan himself; to him will be opposed Enoch and Elias who will return to earth and will convert the Jewish people. Finally during the course of this conflict there will be signs in the sun, the moon and the stars; the earth shall tremble; the sea shall leave its bed, 'and men shall wither away for fear.' (St. Matt. XXIII.) Then the earth shall be swept by an immense fire, and in this general cataclysm the world shall come to an end.

Then will Jesus Christ, the Savior of the world, appear seated upon the clouds—no longer meek and humble as during His mortal life, but in supreme power and majesty, surrounded by millions of angels and resplendent with the glory of God.

At the same time from the various continents, from vanished islands, from the depths of the ocean, from every part of the globe, wherever men have fallen in death, shall rise again the children of Adam; the same infinite Power who created the elements of the body can also reconstitute them in a general resurrection. And it is just, moreover, that man should regain whole and entire his soul and body, in order so to receive the reward or the punishment which he has merited.

There are numbers who in this life knew not Jesus Christ; they shall know Him then. There are many who having followed Him for a time, abandoned Him, perhaps betrayed and persecuted Him; then they shall meet Him again. Many have served and adored Him, in affliction often, in desolation, in poverty, in suffering, in death: they shall see Him also and that hour shall be the hour of their triumph. What a day, what an hour will that be! In an instant shall that tremendous crowd be separated; on the right the good, on the left the wicked. And Jesus Christ will pronounce the final sentence:

"Come," He will say to the good, "ye blessed of my Father, possess ye the kingdom prepared for you from the beginning of the world"; whilst to the wicked He will say: "Depart from me, ye accursed into everlasting fire." (St. Matth. XXV.)

And the separation shall be eternal.

CHAPTER XVIII

LIFE ETERNAL

"AND as it is appointed unto men once to die," says St. Paul "and after this the Judgment" (Heb. IX 27), immediately after death the soul shall find itself in the Presence of God. And in rapid and complete review there shall pass before it all the acts, secret or public, of its whole life, desires, thoughts, all, all. O moment to be dreaded! Instantly judgment is given with such justice as admits of no discussion, and of herself the soul goes to the lot which she has of her own free will chosen—Heaven, or Hell. This is what is called the particular judgment. Every day about 100,000 souls appear thus before the Supreme Judge.

Those souls who on leaving this world are not pure enough to be admitted immediately into Heaven, nor guilty enough to fall into Hell, go to Purgatory, a place where their purification is completed by suffering. In this place of suffering they can no longer merit for themselves, but they are certain of seeing God when their term of penance is ended. They can (it is probable) pray for us, and we can certainly help them. We relieve them by offering for them the Holy Sacrifice of the Mass, by our prayers, our good works, the indulgences which we gain for them.

Hell is the place of eternal torments into which are cast the souls of the damned, that is to say, of those who by their own fault have died deprived of supernatural life, and who at the moment of death and judgment were already separated from God.

In truth, it is in this life and not in the next that, being a spirit and immortal, the human soul must decide upon what is to be its future lot. Its last free wish fixes its destiny, and if it has not wished for God or Heaven, then it shall have neither God nor Heaven; gone astray forever, it shall live in the eternity of misery which it has of its own free will chosen.

The damned suffer a threefold punishment:

They suffer in their total loss of God, — of God for whom they were made and whom they feel they have eternally lost, without the smallest hope of ever being afforded the least glimpse of Him; this is for them unutterable torture (St. Matth. XXV, 41, St. Mark IX, 44, Apoc. XIV, 11, etc.).

They suffer torture of burning by a strange fire, the nature of which is unknown to us, but the reality of which is attested by the Gospel

(St. Matth. XVIII, 25; St. Mark IX; St. Luke, VIII, 16 etc.).

They suffer from remorse, which gnaws them like a worm (St. Mark XVIII, 42), and fills them with indescribable desolation by showing them what they have lost.

How terrific the punishment thus revealed to us! . . . How can we reconcile it with the goodness of God? Undoubtedly it is a mystery. But two things are certain: first, of the existence of Hell we cannot doubt, since Jesus Christ Himself attests it for us: secondly, no one is cast into Hell who has not fully merited it, and never shall any one be able to find a flaw in God's goodness or justice.

Heaven is the abode in which pure souls behold God "face to face" in a happiness, perfect, inexpressible, and which shall never end. In Heaven, as in Hell, for man time no longer exists; for him there are no more hours nor days, nor months nor years: it is eternity.

On earth the good are often unhappy whilst the impious, the wicked, enjoy health, riches, power, honor. Let this pass; to-morrow justice will be reestablished and reign forever.

The "children of the world," says Jesus Christ, are sometimes wiser than the "children of light"; since their habitual thoughts and their constant efforts are all directed to the acquisition of the goods of this world, it is natural that they should succeed. And by granting them the only advantages which they sought, God requites them in this world for the good which they may have done.

But let us, full of hope, take courage and press onward; for Heaven is at the end of our road.

SUMMARY

After the foregoing exposition we now know the whole of the truths which form the object of our Catholic Faith. The Sign of the Cross reminds us of these truths and they are recapitulated in the Apostles' Creed.

THE SIGN OF THE CROSS

In the Name of the Father and of the Son and of the Holy Ghost, Amen.

The Sign of the Cross reminds us that God is One in Three Persons — the Father Who has created us; the Son Who has redeemed us, and the Holy Ghost Who sanctified us by the supernatural life of grace.

In its form — a cross traced upon our body with the right hand — it signifies to us that we have been redeemed on the Cross by the blood of a God, that we are Christians, and that our body is marked for the resurrection and for eternal life.

Finally, the Sign of the Cross is the distinctive mark of Catholic Christians. By tracing it upon ourselves, we assert that we mean to separate ourselves from the infidels, heretics, schismatics, apostates and ex-communicated persons of the whole world, and in the Communion of Saints to unite ourselves forever with the 300 millions of the Faithful of the Catholic Church.

With such sentiments let us often make this sacred sign; let us make it particularly in the morning when we awake, and at night before we fall asleep.

THE APOSTLES' CREED

I believe in God, the Father Almighty, God, the necessary, eternal, infinite, all-powerful Being, Who is everywhere present, and Who sees all things, even the most secret thoughts of our hearts: the Ruler of the Universe, the Father of men, the Providence of the world from Whom nothing escapes, Who, if justice is not done here on earth, will one day restore the balance of justice.

Creator of Heaven and Earth. By an act of His thought and His Will, He has created the whole Universe — invisible beings such as the Angels, and visible beings such as Man. Man composed of a material body destined to be dissolved by death, and a soul spiritual, intelligent and immortal: man whose first representatives were

Adam and Eve, the parents of the human race who fell with them as the result of original sin.

And in Jesus Christ His only Son our Lord, the Messiah, the Christ, the Savior and the Lord of men, God the Son or the Lord.

Who was conceived of the Holy Ghost and born of the Virgin Mary: who — to save the human race and restore to it supernatural life, the friendship of God, and Heaven — was made Man by the mysterious action of the Holy Ghost in the womb of an all pure, immaculate Virgin named Mary.

Suffered under Pontius Pilate, was crucified, dead and buried: having reached manhood, He fulfilled His mission; this mission consisted in making Himself like unto us in all things, even unto suffering and death in order to raise man from his fallen state which was the result of Adam's sin, and to atone for that sin and all the sins which every man has committed, or may commit. So that if I am man and if I have sinned, it is really for me that Jesus Christ under the government of Pontius Pilate suffered in Jerusalem, died, and was committed to the tomb.

He descended into Hell, the third day He rose again from the dead: But He did not remain in the tomb; for, man as He is, He is also God, and He willed to prove this. Having visited the countless souls who throughout the ages had been waiting for Him — on the morning of the third day after His death, during the Feast of the Pasch, He rose again to life.

He ascended into Heaven, sitteth at the right hand of God the Father Almighty: Forty days afterwards, He carried our human nature, which had fallen so low, as high as God, above all creatures visible and invisible. He will reappear. One day this world will come to an end; all the dead shall rise again, and before the assembled millions of the human race, Jesus Christ, the divine Savior, will manifest His power, and with all justice and all mercy will judge every one according to his merits.

I believe in the Holy Ghost: Who gives to all hearts the life of grace which renders us divine on earth whilst we await the hour in which it will render us more completely divine in Heaven.

In the Holy Catholic Church: This life of grace is given to me through the ministry of the holy Catholic Church — the Society organized by Jesus Christ for the salvation of mankind, the Head of which is the Pope, the spiritual Father of all Christians.

The Communion of Saints: As a member of the Catholic Church I belong to the noblest, the most glorious of societies — the Society composed of all those who are united in the supernatural life of grace, of all the friends of God, of all the Saints.

The Forgiveness of sins: By membership in the Church I am also assured that it will be possible for me to obtain remission of my sins. For the Catholic Church has received the power "to bind" and "to loose" on earth all the sins committed by man.

The Resurrection of the Body: And so I advance to my destiny, to death, to the particular Judgment, to the general Resurrection, to Eternal Life.

CHAPTER XIX

CATHOLIC MORALS;   THE UNIVERSAL MORAL LAW

The end of Life — Conscience — Sin — Positive Laws — All morality based on God

WHAT is the supreme end of Man, or in other words: Why are we in this world?   Are we in it only to live like animals? On the answer to this question depends the whole disposition of our life.

"The Lord hath made all things for himself" says holy Scripture (Prov. 16. 4). "He is the *Alpha* and the *Omega*, the first and the last," the beginning and the end of all. But this is not because the marvels of Creation could have added anything to His infinite perfection. The Creation is but the radiation of His goodness and a certain communication of Himself which He gives to His creatures.

Man is irresistibly impelled towards happiness. He may be mistaken and he often is mistaken in his idea of happiness, but yet he is always in pursuit of it; it is his last end and aim, towards which he ever tends and on which he must concentrate his mind. All other aims are subordinated to this one.

Now this happiness cannot consist of any finite good — strength, health, riches, pleasure, honors, science or even virtue; for nothing of all this is lasting or can satisfy the human heart. The human heart can only be satisfied by the possession, acquired once and forever, of Truth, of Goodness and of Beauty.

Now in God alone can be found universal Truth, supreme Goodness and absolute Beauty. Therefore it is in God that man must seek his last end and his perfect happiness. Hence that beautiful saying of St. Augustine, "Thou hast made us for Thyself, O God, and in Thee alone shall our hearts find rest."

But how shall man attain to this end?

Being supremely perfect, God wills that order and righteousness should rule His Work. Hence He has made the whole of Creation subject to a law or rule to which it must conform. This Eternal Law governs everything absolutely, whilst varying in the different orders of Creation — inert matter, living creatures, rational beings. Inert matter is governed by the laws of astronomy, mechanics, physics, chemistry, etc., from which, unless by intervention of the Creator, it does not deviate. In the same way living things, plants and animals fulfil their end according to the biological laws imposed on them.

Finally the rational being, Man, who is governed in that part of him which is inert and that which is animal by the preceding laws, is, besides, subject to a higher law which is imposed on his intellect and his will; this law is called Moral Law. Such is the order, the supreme order which reigns in the whole of Creation.

This order is not disturbed either by inert matter or living matter, but it can be disturbed by man. For God, in order that he may gain merit has made man free. And it is this disorder voluntarily introduced by man into the universal order which constitutes *Sin*.

Christian perfection, on the contrary, has no other end or aim than to maintain man from the cradle to the grave in continual submission to this higher order. It is conscience which imposes on the individual this Moral Law. But as in the divine plans it is arranged that to form the Family, individuals be associated together, and as in the same manner to form Society, families must be associated together, the Moral Law in its application to this classification will vary in its express rules — whether of a religious or civil or political or social nature. And if they are in accordance with order, all these laws under different titles and varying degrees will be of obligation.

These clear and simple ideas which present within its own limits each of the elements of the Creation, apply to all the developments which follow.

Let us recapitulate them.

Animals know what is good and what is bad for them by a realization purely transient of their destiny, but they have no idea of the morality of their acts, they are not responsible for them; they are not moral agents. Hence of them it may be said with truth: "once they are dead, everything has died with them." With their life their destiny is ended.

With man it is quite different. For him the present life is but a preparation for the life to come. It is a voyage which must terminate at a port. It is a trial which will have its sanction.

And this is why man feels himself responsible for his actions; his conscience enlightens him, prompts him, restrains him, approves, blames, fills him with satisfaction, with sadness or remorse, according to the case; by his conduct he gains merit or demerit; [1] he has the perception of moral good or evil, and he feels that this good as well as this evil must have a sanction either

[1] Merit is the right to a reward, demerit entails the obligation of submitting to punishment.

in this world or in the next. His destiny is determined in eternity.

Such in effect is the will of the Creator regarding His intelligent creatures: eternal happiness in the vision and love of God, acquired by his own free will with the supernatural assistance of God's grace. This is the one and only thing necessary; all that helps us to this end is good; all that diverts us from it is evil. The science of life, therefore, consists simply in making God our end and aim, in tending towards Him as towards the Supreme Ideal given to all creatures according to the rule formulated by Jesus Christ Himself and in which the whole Moral Law is summed up: "Be ye perfect, as your heavenly Father is perfect."

This rule of human life, or universal Moral Law, being of obligation, must be known by every man, but it rests with himself to decide whether he will obey it or not, for Providence wills that he should be free. And for this reason God proclaims it to every man by showing it to him in that sort of interior light which is called Conscience or the Moral Sense. Hence the name of Natural Law has been given to this universal Moral Law because it is innate in human nature.[1]

However, no more than physical strength or

[1] *Conscience*, in Latin, *conscientia*, from *conscius*, knowing in oneself.

intelligence, is conscience the same in every one; according to the persons or the circumstances it seems to be more or less right or wrong, assured or faltering, enlightened or ignorant, lax, rigid or scrupulous. Our duty is, so far as we can do so, to keep it in good order and to obey it.

From the depths of our nature it is true, there arise other voices than that of upright judgment: the voices of pride, of sensuality, of envy, which tempt us — that is to say, which incite us to do wrong. But in spite of all that we remain free, and nothing can make us deviate from the right path unless we wish to do so. If, therefore, we resist the temptation, we draw down upon us the blessing of God and we become stronger; but if we yield to it, we commit sin, and after sin come sadness and remorse. Next, perhaps, we shall have acquired the habit of sin; and this may end in our forsaking God and losing Him forever.

Sin may be either slight or grave, venial or mortal.

Venial sin — that is to say, sin that may be easily forgiven, offends God in small matters, or it may be in grave ones committed without our full knowledge, will, or consent. It weakens and tends to paralyze supernatural life, but does not destroy it; it does not directly diminish sanctifying grace in the soul; it does not turn us away from our last end or aim.

Mortal sin, that is the sin which causes the death of the supernatural life in our souls, is an offense against God in grave matters, committed with full knowledge and deliberation; it turns us away from our end.

In order that a human action may be good or evil, it must result from our free and conscious will. The act of a man who is heedless, inattentive to what he is doing, sleepy, delirious, intoxicated, ignorant of the goodness or the malice of the act committed, dominated by fear, constrained by force, in a word deprived in any way whatsoever of the free use of his intelligence or his will, is no longer the act of a human being; therefore it only admits of merit or demerit in proportion to the measure of intelligence or of will which was concerned in its production.

The natural Law being liable, having regard to human nature, to become obscured and distorted, and on the other hand man not having been made to lead an isolated life, it was fitting that God, whether of Himself or by authorized legislators, should take care to set it forth clearly, and to regulate its various applications with a view to determining the rights and the duties of the individual, of the Family, and of Society.

This is why we have *positive laws*, so called because they are imposed by a positive act of the law-giver. But they derive their obligatory force from the Natural Law, which is itself the expression of God's thought and Will.

The religious positive laws comprise: The Ancient or Mosaic Law, given by God to Moses for the Jewish people, abolished in that part relating solely to ceremonial by our divine Lord.

The New Law or Law of the Gospel, promulgated by Jesus Christ for all men; in which Law are included the theological precepts, that is, the whole of the religious truths which we must believe.

The moral precepts or the commandments which we must obey, beginning with the Commandments of God or the Decalogue, which, not being given solely for the Jewish people, were confirmed by our divine Savior.

The Sacramental precepts, or the Sacraments, which are intended to communicate to us sanctifying grace, to maintain it within us, or, should we have lost it, to restore it to us.

To these precepts are added the Evangelical Counsels given with regard to the acquiring of Christian perfection and which are adapted to a special state of life — the Religious life.

Finally, in order to regulate, to state clearly and to facilitate the fulfilment of the Law of the Gospel, the Church, acting in the name and with the power of her divine Founder, has also made laws, called ecclesiastical laws or Commandments of the Church which are binding on all Catholics.

Furthermore; as men are formed to live in company with their fellow men, it is necessary for the maintenance of peace and order that their relations with one another and their interests should be controlled by civil and political laws, always in harmony with the Moral Law over which nothing must prevail.

But to impose a law in this manner upon men supposes a Ruler. And, as in its essential prescription this Moral Law applies to all men, in all ages, countries and races, individually as well as collectively, governing not only their exterior or public conduct but even their most secret actions, their intentions and their thoughts, this Ruler must be the Supreme Ruler of the world, He Who "searches the reins and the heart", He Who is prepared to reward or to punish adequately every act, every design, done or conceived of man's free will.

This is why Reason agrees with Faith in recognizing that Morality can be based on the Will of God alone, a Will infinitely just, which is expressed by Himself or by His authorized representatives.

Any other conception which would render Morality independent of Religion and of the Divinity; any force of which we are unconscious, mere social conventions, joint interests (mutual responsibility), ancient customs, or simple prepossessions, is an impossible conception. A law founded on such basis would be obligatory on no one, and could only be imposed by force. The Moral Law, as we understand it, on the contrary, being imposed by God, is of obligation on all men alike.

Is there anything greater, simpler, clearer, more reasonable, more admirable, than this Catholic conception of morality and law?

Is there anything which could insure more liberty to man, more dignity to the Family, more peace to Society?

CHAPTER XX

THE NATURAL LAW

Virtues and Vices

THE natural Law is framed on the Will of God itself; it is universal; it is unalterable; it is of obligation for every one, apart from any motive of interest; it is independent of our will, and, like all efficacious laws, it carries with it a sanction either in this world or the next. No one can be exempt from it, and all human laws contrary to it must be regarded as null and void.

The natural Law imposes a certain number of general obligations, such as: to acknowledge and to honor God as the Creator, the Ruler, and the Universal Law-giver Who commands us to do good and to avoid evil, to respect our own nature, not to do to others what we should not wish to be done to ourselves; etc.

The application of these principles may vary according to the time, the country, and the circumstances; they remain, notwithstanding, the basis of the universal Moral Law.

Natural moral sense has become enriched with various developments, and in the first place with certain ideas which must be connected with the primitive Revelation and with the most ancient traditions of the human race. Then there are hereditary and family influences and lessons as well as those of education, of environment, of personal experience. Thus it happens that in the countries long permeated by Christianity, many of those who appear hostile or indifferent to all religious belief live nevertheless to a great extent on an inheritance of Christianity which, without their being conscious of it, exercises on them an all-pervading influence.

Self-respect, a sense of justice, honesty, loyalty, fidelity to one's word, courage, kindness, devotion to one's family and to society, patriotism, etc.; such are the virtues which serve as basis for this general moral law in the natural order and which practised without any higher motive, constitute what all agree to call natural goodness. And this basis is necessary; any attempt to build up religious perfection on any other foundation would be a mere delusion or contemptible hypocrisy.

But it would not suffice for a man to be only a decent-living infidel. God has made us for Himself. Now we cannot belong to Him unless we live the supernatural life to which we are all called.

This is the reason that by the will of God man is bound to seek Him, to know Him, to adhere to His Word by Faith (which will be given to every one who has the necessary dispositions), and at the same time be prepared to give up everything which would absolutely prevent him from attaining to his supreme end.

He is bound, therefore, to put himself in a state of grace by sincere sorrow for his faults, and by receiving, if not already baptized, the Sacrament of Baptism. By Baptism he becomes a member of the family of Jesus Christ and is set on the way of eternal salvation. He is bound afterwards to lead a Christian life, to maintain himself in the state of grace by the observance of the Commandments of God and the Church, by prayer and participation in divine worship. He is bound, finally, if by committing grave sin he should happen to turn away from his supreme end, to return to "the Way, the Truth and the Life" by Penance and by receiving the Sacraments which Jesus Christ has instituted to give to souls supernatural life and to maintain it within them. This is a summary of the moral life, as it must be understood and realized in order that man may attain to his true end — union with God on earth and afterwards in the happiness of heaven.

We have seen that the morality of our actions

depends upon the intentions with which they are performed. If the intention is purely natural, excluding all thought of religion, these actions, no doubt, may be good, but they avail us nothing for the attainment of our end which is God.

In order that our actions may count in the balance wherein must be decided our eternal destiny, the intention animating them must be supernatural — that is, inspired by Faith, and they must be sanctified by habitual grace. It is not necessary that this motive should be formally expressed; it suffices that we are in a state of grace and in the general disposition to live in conformity with the Will of God. The desire to renew and revive this disposition is the reason of the Christian practise which consists in offering every morning the actions of the day to our Creator.

The habit of acting according to the dictates of an upright conscience is called *Virtue*. This word comes from the Latin *virtus* which means "manliness." The virtuous man is, indeed the true man — he who knows how to will, to govern his evil inclinations and to conquer himself. It is for such alone, says Jesus Christ, that the Kingdom is reserved.

The three great Christian virtues called theological, that is, divine, because they relate directly to God are Faith, Hope and Charity.

By Faith we believe — that is, we hold as certain all that God has revealed and that He proposes to us through the Catholic Church; and we believe, not because we understand, but because God has said it and He can speak only the truth.

Hence Faith is meritorious, because it is, above all, an humble submission of our understanding to the sovereign authority of God. But whilst proposing to us mysteries which are beyond our comprehension, God does not impose on us any which are contrary to reason, impossible or absurd, and He even confirms those He proposes by innumerable proofs. Our holy Religion, therefore, is at once *rational* and *deserving of reward*.

The foundation of the whole Christian life is Faith; without it, "it is impossible to please God" (Heb. XI. 6). To proclaim it simply and freely, and if necessary, to suffer and die for it; this is the Christian's greatest honor.

The principal sins against Faith are: Indifference, which renders a man careless about seeking and practising the true Religion; voluntary doubt and unbelief, which close the mind to religious truth; Superstition, which causes confidence to be placed in vain and forbidden practises; Heresy, which confirms in men's minds the errors condemned by the Church; Apostasy, by which men abandon and deny the Catholic Faith. All these states of mind arise commonly from the following causes: ignorance of the Catholic Religion, pride of intellect, weakness of will, sensuality of heart, disorderly lives.

By Hope we count firmly on the goodness of God that He will give us eternal salvation with the graces necessary to attain it, for He is faithful to His promises (Heb. X. 23). This blessed virtue produces peace in our soul, patience and Christian resignation, interior joy and the desire of heavenly things, and happiness on earth as far as happiness can be enjoyed on earth.

The sins against Hope are two: Presumption, which causes us to think that we can be saved by God's goodness alone, without giving ourselves any trouble about the Commandments; and Despair, which drives man to think that God has abandoned him and that he is lost eternally, and to act as if this were so.

Charity is the most perfect of the virtues. It is a supernatural impulse of the soul which urges us to unite ourselves to God as to the Supreme Good, the ineffable Beauty, the infinite Goodness, to love Him above all things, to sacrifice everything that we may remain faithful to Him.

The same supernatural impulse urges us to love the rational creatures whom He has made; to lead them to Him; to help them; to do good to their souls and to their bodies.

The true proof that we have this love for God

is our fidelity in leading a Christian life fear-
lessly and without yielding to weakness.

All mortal sins are contrary to Charity. With
regard to hatred of God, this can only be the sin
of Satan and of those possessed by him. How
can a rational human being hate God!

The other virtues are called *moral virtues* because they directly tend to regulate our manners
or conduct in conformity with our supreme end.

Of these virtues the four principal or cardinal
ones are: Prudence, Justice, Fortitude and Temperance.

Prudence consists in knowing how to discern
what is good and what is evil, what we should do
and what we should avoid.

Justice, in rendering to every man what is due
to him.

Fortitude, in doing one's duty with courage and
constancy, let what will happen.

Temperance, in using things with moderation.

We have said that deliberate and voluntary
transgression of a law of God constitutes *Sin*.

The habit of sin in such or such a matter is a
Vice.

The principal Vices, called the seven Capital
Sins, are: Pride, Avarice, Lust, Envy, Gluttony,
Anger, Sloth. They are called capital (that is
chief) from the word *caput*, head, because they
are, as it were, the head or the cause of all other

sins. Let us cut off the heads, and the "Beast" will perish.

These vices, when they are grave, deprive us of grace, cause us to lose the merit of our good works, often ruin health and fortune, leave the soul no rest, and make of a man a veritable slave who knows neither peace nor happiness.

Let us examine ourselves well in order to find out our predominant fault. Is it pride? Is it sensuality? Is it sloth?

The principal means for our reformation are: to resist from the beginning our criminal inclinations, to live in the presence of God, to be active and hard-working, to avoid bad company, to be moderate in eating and drinking, to go often to Confession and to Holy Communion, and no matter what happens, never to give up the faithful practise of our Religion.

Let us be strong against ourselves.

CHAPTER XXI

THE DECALOGUE

A T the same time that God confided the great truths of Religion to the custody of the posterity of Abraham, of Isaac, and of Jacob, He willed to determine the essential elements of the natural Law, always liable to be misunderstood or distorted. Therefore He gave them written on two tables of stone to Moses, the Leader of the Jewish people; these are known as the Decalogue or Ten Commandments.[1]

This promulgation of the Law took place three months after the Hebrews, having quitted Egypt, had begun their journeying towards Palestine. Whilst they were encamped at the foot of Mount Sinai, Moses was called to ascend the mountain, and there he received the divine code amidst thunder and lightning, which invested this promulgation with a solemn and impressive grandeur.

Afterwards Jesus Christ being come upon the

---

[1] From the Greek, δέκα, ten, and λόγοι, sayings.

earth "not to destroy the law — but to fulfil" (Matth. 5. 17) He promulgated anew these Commandments, perfected the Old Law, and committed it to the guardianship of His Church with the mission to make it known with the truths of Faith to all men.

And it is the combination of these which constitutes the New or the Christian Law.

The Ten Commandments as given in Holy Scripture are as follows:

1. I am the Lord thy God; thou shalt not have strange gods before Me.

2. Thou shalt not take the name of the Lord thy God in vain.

3. Remember that thou keep holy the Sabbath day.

4. Honor thy father and thy mother.

5. Thou shalt not kill.

6. Thou shalt not commit adultery.

7. Thou shalt not steal.

8. Thou shalt not bear false witness against thy neighbor.

9. Thou shalt not covet thy neighbor's wife.

10. Thou shalt not covet thy neighbor's goods.

(Exod. XX, Deut. V.)

As we see, the first three Commandments written on the first table of stone, determine our duties to God; the fourth, our duties to our families, the basis of all Society; the six others, our duties to ourselves and to our neighbor.

Our Lord has summed them up in those two admirable precepts which contain the whole of Christian Morality and constitute the Law of Charity. 1st. To love God, our Supreme Good, above all things and for Himself alone. 2nd. To love our neighbor as ourselves, in God, and because of God, our Master in all things and our common Father.

These two precepts are at once natural and positive, and have a comprehension as extended as the divine code itself.

The Commandments given to Moses, on the contrary — that was the law of fear — have in general a prohibitive form; there is vaster scope for good than for evil. All that is not forbidden is permitted; all that is permitted has a relation to the end of man: and all that furthers, directly or indirectly, the end of man, is a good.

Since this code of ten Laws, so simple, so reasonable, so adapted to the requirements of Nature were formulated, more than 3,000 years have passed. Since then nothing better has ever been devised by the wisdom of man. And the strict observance of the Decalogue, if practised, would suffice to insure the happiness of the individual, of the Family, of Society.

If it makes no proclamation of our rights, by

prescribing for us our duties it perfectly assures respect for those rights; for if each one fulfils his duties, the rights of all will be guaranteed. Let individuals, families, Society, each and all return to the observance of the Decalogue, if they would secure happiness and prosperity.

CHAPTER XXII

I

OUR DUTIES TOWARDS GOD: TO ADORE HIM: TO RESPECT HIS NAME; TO RESPECT HIS DAY

I am the Lord thy God; thou shalt not have strange Gods before me.

IN the first three Commandments we learn our duties towards God.

The First Commandment commands us to adore God only, to serve Him and to love Him above all things, and never to offend Him by impiety, indifference, neglect or superstition. He is our Creator; He is our Lord and Master; He is our Father; *Pater Noster*. To adore God is to acknowledge that God alone possesses these sovereign qualities, and consequently to render to Him the Worship which He demands from us, and which the Catholic Church in her own commandments has arranged for us.

The Son of God being made Man, we must adore Jesus Christ as God, in His Body, His Blood,

His Heart, because in Him Man and God are but one and the same Person.

We do not adore, but we honor — as we honor our father, our mother, our protectors, our friends — the Blessed Virgin Mary, the Angels and the Saints. From God alone we ask grace and mercy; from the Saints we only ask the assistance of their prayers.

We may also reproduce the likeness of the Saints who are the friends of God, for God has not said "thou shalt not make images," but "Thou shalt not *adore* them, nor *serve* them." (Exod. XX. 5; Levit. XXVI, 1; Deut. V. 9.)

It is in this same spirit that Catholics carry about them blessed objects, medals and crucifixes, and that they venerate the Cross and the relics of the Saints.

In themselves these objects have no power, no virtue, but because of the blessing of the Church whereby they have been sanctified, we venerate them, as well also as because of that which they recall to us and what they represent to us.

Finally Jesus Christ, our divine Savior, is the sole Mediator between God and Men. Only as the friends and servants of God do we appeal to the Saints. Was it not thus that the first disciples appealed to the Apostles of Christ in order that they might have access to Him? This simple truth Protestants refuse to understand.

Amongst the sins forbidden by the First Commandment let us mention first of all impiety, sacrilege, despair, paganism, indifference or neglect of religion, in fine, every thought, word or action against Religion: for Religion is the acknowledgement and service of God.

To sin by impiety is, for example, voluntarily to remain a pagan or an infidel, to be attached to heresy, to apostacy, or to abandon the Catholic Religion, to be ashamed of being a Catholic, of saying one's prayers, of going to Mass and of practising one's Religion. This is a miserable cowardice. Our Divine Lord has said of it these terrible words:—

"But he that shall deny me before men, I will also deny him before my Father who is in Heaven" (Matth. X. 33).

To commit sacrilege is to profane or treat with disrespect holy things—the Sacraments, churches, cemeteries, sacred vessels, objects of piety; to ill-treat priests or Religious; to steal Church property.

To despair of God and our salvation, like Cain and Judas, is a sin, as is also to continue in wrongdoing, saying that God will save us notwithstanding.

It is also a sin to show indifference or to be neglectful in matters of Religion. In reality, without expressly denying God, the indifferent man lives as if God did not exist; this is to insult Him continually.

Paganism is to render worship to other beings than God, for instance to offer prayers, or sacrifices to the demons, to evil spirits, to the spirits of the dead; to consult soothsayers, to employ witch-craft, to wear amulets or pretended charms in order to be preserved from harm; to venerate fetishes; to take part in heathen dances; to give oneself to superstitious practises, to spiritism, to magic.

Finally we are forbidden to join secret societies, such as that of the Free-Masons, the hidden end of which is to combat the Christian Religion, and similar societies established to maintain the errors and the practises of infidels.

Even in those regions in which Christianity has been established for ages, the world tends to return to infidelity.

How many people, even in the great centers of Europe and America, are destitute of all idea of religion; have no other morality than that which suits them; have no other thought than "to live their life," know no other end to existence than that of the animals about them. How many have not even been baptized!

Others comply with certain rites, at times of birth, of marriage, of death, but remain practically blind and deaf as far as regards all supernatural ideas.

Others are deliberately anti-Christian. This is a retrogression from civilization.

Now to punish a people which abandons Him, God does not need to act towards them as an angry master; it suffices for Him to leave them to their errors, to their depravity, to their follies.

To sum up: God wills that we should adore Him alone. For He is the Master and the Father. To place our confidence in any other being is an insult to Him; it is rendering honor to imaginary beings, or beings who have no power whatever; it may result in our placing ourselves in the power of the devil, who since his fall from Heaven seeks to take the place of God on earth.

II

RESPECT FOR THE NAME OF GOD

Thou shalt not take the name of the Lord thy God in vain

By the second Commandment we are forbidden to offend God in His Name by language which is insulting, false, or unjust (S. Matth. 5, 34; S. James, 5, 12.)

"Be not deceived," says St. Paul, "God is not mocked" (Gal. III. 7). Of this we are reminded by the second Commandment.

Now, we should "mock God,"—

1. By wilfully using insulting or blasphemous language towards God, the servants of God, or the things of God. The Jews punished the sin of blasphemy with death;

2. By swearing, that is by invoking the most Holy Name of God in a moment of anger or in ordinary conversation, as so many have the habit of doing,—this, strictly speaking, is not blasphemy but a gross way of speaking which should be avoided.

3. Scoffing at Religion and holy things; speaking ill of priests and Religious, or approving of such talk, and being afraid to profess our Religion from cowardice or human respect.

4. Cursing the works of God, by wishing death or any evil whatsoever to ourselves or to others.

5. Declaring on oath as true something which we know to be false, especially before a judge: this is what is called perjury. But when we are called upon, in justice, to tell the truth, we are permitted to take God as the witness of the truths of what we say, either directly (as for instance, by saying "I swear before God") or indirectly by putting our hand on the New Testament — this is called an oath, and it imposes on us a grave obligation to tell the truth.

6. Breaking our vows, — that is, neglecting or refusing to fulfil them. A vow is a promise made

to God with the intention of being bound by conscience to perform some good work, such as to give an alms, to say prayers, to make a pilgrimage. If the performance of our vow proves impossible, its obligation ceases; if unforeseen difficulties arise, we ought to apply to our confessor, and may ask him to change it, or to dispense us from its observance.

We should be careful not make vows lightly.

III

THE LORD'S DAY

Remember that thou keep holy the Sabbath Day

The third Commandment of God commands us to be faithful in sanctifying the Lord's day — namely Sunday.

In Holy Scripture God is represented as working "six days" in the creation and organization of the world. On the seventh day he "rested." The days of God are not as the days of man, but by this great example, a lesson is given to man from the moment in which he takes possession of the world to cease from work on one day out of seven in order to fulfil his duties towards God. This is the institution of the week, of which the greatness and importance are revealed in its divine origin thus established.

Amongst the Jews Saturday was appointed as

this day of rest and prayer. This the Apostles changed to Sunday in honor of our Lord's Resurrection at Easter and the foundation of the Church at Pentecost, both of which took place on Sunday (Act, XX, 7; I Cor. XVI. 2).

On this day unless under pressing necessity, all heavy work is forbidden to us. It is also forbidden to us to make our workmen or servants work. Such labor is what is called servile work or manual labor, which is chiefly done by bodily exertion, in contradistinction to mental work. Walking, traveling, hunting, etc. and other exercises of a similar kind are not considered servile work.

But this does not suffice. We must also honor God by sacrifice. Now in the Christian Law the Mass is the Sacrifice which takes the place of all others. This is the great Sacrifice, stainless, priceless, of God to God for humanity, offered on thousands of altars for the worshipers who assemble round them. Unless from necessity, such as the duties of our state in life, sickness, traveling, or too great distance from the church, we are not dispensed from assisting at this Sacrifice. When unable to be present, we ought to make up for our loss by praying at home.

God blesses the people and families who keep holy the Sabbath Day. Sunday is indeed the Lord's Day; let us not filch it from Him.

Let us add that this law regarding Sunday is preeminently a social law. Man has need of a day of rest every week, in order to recruit his strength and to enjoy life sanely — not only the material life, but the life of the soul, of the intellect, and of the heart; to experience in peace the joy of family life; from time to time to raise his eyes towards Heaven, and not to be always bowed down, like an animal, towards earth and the things of earth.

Besides, experience has proved that Sunday labor is good neither for individuals, nor the family, nor the nation. It brutalizes them without enriching them.

CHAPTER XXIII

THE DECALOGUE

IV

OUR DUTIES TOWARDS OUR FAMILIES

Honor thy father and thy mother

BY this fourth Commandment of God we are ordered to render honor and respect to our parents and to all superiors in general.

In other terms God imposes upon us as a duty to respect the family, such as He has willed it to be from the beginning. The family is the fundamental institution; all that weakens it, corrupts it, disorganizes it, weakens, corrupts and disorganizes the nation and society.

To honor our father and our mother is to respect them, to love them, to obey them, and to help them in poverty, in sickness, in old age. It also means to be anxious for the salvation of their souls, to procure for them the last Sacraments when necessary, to pray for them during their lifetime and after death. The child who loves its parents will have the blessing of God; the one who forgets them, ill-treats or dishonors them, shall be accursed. (Levit. XX. 9; Col. III. 20.)

However, if parents should command their children to do something contrary to Religion, seeking to draw them into forbidden actions, to lead them away from their duties, or obliging them to live in a state of sin, Christian children must firmly refuse. For God must be obeyed rather than men (Acts, 11, 29).

On the other hand parents must bring up their children, by taking care of their souls and bodies, by feeding them, clothing them, teaching them their religion, instructing them, accustoming them to work; helping to start them in life, preventing them from acquiring bad habits, correcting them, praying for them, and by never saying or doing anything wrong in their presence. Parents who by their neglect allow their children to be lost are accomplices in their sins and the cause of their damnation. (Prov. XIII. 84; Eph. VI. 4).

Parents are also obliged, as a grave obligation in conscience, to see that their children receive a virtuous, Christian training. To corrupt a child's heart and mind by a godless education is a crime, for it ends in the eternal loss of souls. How can parents have any part in such an awful thing?

It is scarcely necessary to say how guilty in the

sight of God parents would be, if they themselves corrupted their children and made them lead evil lives. At the hour of death they would have to answer for the loss of these immortal souls committed to their care.

This Commandment also obliges dependents and servants to obey and to respect their masters. On their part masters should take care of their dependents and servants; they should give them what is due to them, treat them with kindness and justice and see that all under them are instructed in their religion.

They have no right to prevent them fulfilling their duties by refusing them, for example, the Sunday rest, unless in cases of downright necessity (Col. III. 22, IV. 1; Eph. VI. 5).

The same thing applies to teachers; they are bound to give their pupils good example and good lessons, and to respect conscience, the moral law and religion.

The State, which is the union of all the natives of the same country, has a right to our cooperation. For the duty of the State is to insure the existence, the freedom, the defense, and the prosperity of the country, which is as it were an extension of the family. We should be patriots, contributing to the maintenance of peace and order, working for good, taking our share of taxation and faithfully fulfilling our duties as citizens.

The State on its side, in the persons of those who represent it, is obliged to respect the rights and liberties of our Christian consciences (I. St. Peter, II. 13–14; Rom. XIII. 1–7; Acts V. 29). Not to do so is to be guilty of the worst tyranny.

The Church is a mother, and all Christians are her children; it is she, in truth, who gives them and maintains in them supernatural life through the grace of the Sacraments. Hence they should obey her, love, respect, defend, and assist her according to their means, and contribute to the propagation of her faith which is ours also.

The Church also has her duties for which she is responsible in the sight of God.

CHAPTER XXIV

THE DECALOGUE

OUR DUTIES TOWARDS SOCIETY

HAVING determined our duties to God and to our families, the Decalogue settles our duties towards Society of which God is also the Author.

But we ourselves are in this regard the principal members of Society; so that the six last commandments of God in an admirable gradation which comprises life, material goods, and moral good, prescribe the respect which we should have for our own souls and bodies and those of our neighbors, that is for the souls and bodies of all those with whom we have any connection.

V

Thou shalt not kill

It is from God that we all hold our life. The fifth Commandment forbids us to injure this life either in ourselves or others.

Therefore man is forbidden to kill himself —

commit suicide. We have no right to take our own life, for it belongs to Him Who gave it to us, that is, to God. By suicide man flings his soul burdened with a horrible crime into the hands of the Eternal Judge — What fate can there be reserved for him? But when it is a question of self-sacrifice for others, in case of war, of pestilence, of fire, not only is he allowed to expose himself to danger of death, but he who does so imitates the devotedness of Jesus Christ Who "laid down His life for us" (John 3. 16).

Homicide is the killing of man by man, committed wilfully and without any special mandate from the lawful and competent authorities. It is a crime which cries to Heaven for vengeance; every assassin draws down on himself the malediction which smote Cain.

To commit the sin of murder, let us remark, it is not necessary that the victim should be in the full vigor of manhood or womanhood; it suffices to put to death any human being, no matter in what way, even to a child not yet come to the use of reason, even an unborn infant.

And should we not here allude to those truly homicidal practices which in certain countries have caused such a decline in the population as to alarm all right-minded people? Empty homes, deserted villages, families committing suicide: what can be sadder, more alarming for the future, above all more contrary to the designs of the Creator and to the first orders which He gave?

Duel-fighting is also a grave sin, as is also the ill-treatment of any one, striking or wounding, taking revenge, harboring malice or hatred etc.

However, if a person is attacked by an enemy or a thief, he can defend himself and repulse his assailant even by the use of force; this is what is called a case of legitimate defense. If this enemy menaces the whole nation in aggressive war, then the whole nation has the right, and its government has the duty, to resist the aggressor, to uphold its rights and to keep its freedom.

Our neighbor's supernatural life has to suffer in particular from scandal. Scandal is everything bad which said or done before others is capable of drawing them into sin. Thus to turn others from the practise of Religion; to give bad advice; to hold bad conversations; to lend bad books, to sing bad songs; to entice others to unseemly dances, to tempt them to debauchery: all these are scandals by which you lose your own soul, and also the soul of a brother who will reproach you eternally for his damnation. Our divine Savior has specially anathematized those who give scandal to the innocent souls of children. "But he that shall scandalize one of these little ones that believe in me, it were better for him that a millstone should be hanged about his neck, and that he should be drowned in the depth of the sea." (St. Matth. XVIII. 6.)

The father or the mother of a family who does not pray, who does not go to Mass on Sunday or who neglects the Easter duty, by giving this bad example and this lamentable lesson to his or her children is particularly guilty.

It does not suffice for a Christian merely to refrain doing harm to others; he must endeavor by works of mercy to do them good.

The Spiritual Works of Mercy are:

To counsel the doubtful,
To instruct the ignorant,
To admonish sinners,
To comfort the afflicted,
To forgive offenses,
To bear wrongs patiently,
To pray for the living and the dead.

Corporal Works of Mercy:

To feed the hungry,
To give drink to the thirsty,
To clothe the naked,
To harbor the harborless,
To visit the sick,
To visit the captive, and
To bury the dead.

VI

Thou shalt not commit adultery

IX

Thou shalt not covet thy neighbor's wife

The Sixth Commandment of God which is completed by the ninth, bidding us respect in ourselves and in others all that concerns the propagation of the human race forbids all acts, words, reading, desires or thoughts contrary to purity.

The importance of this divine precept is evident. By it Providence associates each one of us with the great work of guarding the continuance of man's mission upon earth and the constant succession of souls and bodies destined to eternal glory.   Equally plain is the gravity of the offense when man perverts the well-springs of life into occasions of selfish degrading pleasures, and prefers a transitory animal pleasure to the designs and will of his Creator.

The sins against this Commandment are therefore always grave when committed with full consent and deliberation.   The Apostle St. Paul, tells us that they should not even be mentioned amongst Christians.   "Or know you not, he writes, that your members are the temple of the Holy

Ghost, who is in you, whom you have from God; and you are not your own?" (1 Cor. III. 19.)

Indulgence in any of them separates the unhappy sinner from God, from peace of mind. The heart grows hardened; faith fades and dies; the mental powers are dulled and sometimes ruined, for no other sin drags down man so completely to the level of the brute. The body itself pays the penalty, and sometimes terribly.

Let us avoid bad friends; bad conversations; bad songs; bad reading; let us keep away from bad plays; above all let parents watch over their children. For the Holy Ghost tells us that "he who loves the danger shall perish in it." (Eccles. III. 24.)

What is necessary in order not to yield to temptation? 1. Drive away evil thoughts at once, do not dwell on them; occupy yourself with something that will distract you. 2. Pray fervently to our Lady. 3. Go often to Confession and to Holy Communion. 4. Always observe modesty in your words, your dress, and your looks. 5. Abstain from alcoholic drinks and avoid all excess in eating or drinking. 6. Work. 7. Try in all you do to be energetic and active; fly the occasions of sin; be determined and of strong will. Respect yourself.

It must be added that in these matters as in all others thoughts or imagination which merely

pass through the mind, which we have not voluntarily caused, on which we do not deliberately
dwell, are not sins. For the commission of any
sin there must be always consent of the will.

Those who preserve purity of heart will always
enjoy a source of true happiness for they are
truly free and friends of God. Those who neglect this purity of heart are slaves to desires
which never leave them at rest; they never know
peace of soul, and know not the meaning of happiness. "Blessed are the pure in heart, for they
shall see God." (St. Matth. V. 8.)

VII

Thou shalt not steal

X

Thou shalt not covet thy neighbor's goods

By these two Commandments we are forbidden
not only to appropriate to ourselves our neighbor's goods, but even to desire to possess them
unjustly.

There are several ways of stealing or of wronging others. Thus to take something by force;
by cunning and stratagem; to cheat in buying
or selling; to prosecute any one unjustly; to neglect
payment of one's debts; to lend money at too
high a rate of interest; not to return money or

things borrowed; to refuse payment due to those who work for us; to squander the property of others; to keep stolen goods; to take payment for work we have not done; to take part in a robbery; to assist or to hide a thief; to cause loss to any one even by not keeping one's word or by not carrying out a contract: all this is forbidden by God Who has said "Thou shalt not steal."

Let us remark here that to be quits with our conscience and to discharge our debt to God and our neighbor, it will not suffice to accuse ourselves in Confession of having committed theft or injured our neighbor in his property; we must also return what we have taken and make restitution, as far as we can, for the loss we have occasioned.

Without restitution there can be no forgiveness.

Stolen goods call for their owner; if he is dead or cannot be found, then we must give them or cause them to be given to the family, and failing this, they must be given to the poor or to some good work. Finally, if we have not the means to pay back all that we have taken, we must give according to our means.

"Ill-gotten goods seldom prosper." God, Who is the Master of all, will see that justice is done.

All thefts and all injuries done, obviously, are not of equal gravity; some are trifling, some may be very serious. The degree of our own need will make a difference in our guilt; so will the degree in which the loser feels the loss.

It is a twofold sin to steal Church property, or anything else consecrated to God; there is the sin of theft and furthermore sacrilege is committed.

The tenth Commandment does not forbid us to work with the view of improving our condition and that of our families. Far from it. But it condemns that inordinate desire of wealth which is capable of leading us into the greatest misfortune; it was by this that Judas, the avaricious and traitorous Apostle was lost eternally; he sold his Master for thirty pieces of silver and immediately afterwards hanged himself in despair. From this inordinate desire of wealth proceed avarice which is an excessive craving for the goods of this world; usury or the imposition of an exorbitant rate for the loan of money; hard-heartedness towards the unfortunate, fraud in buying and selling, and in general, all that is contrary to honesty.

Nor is it forbidden to desire juster laws and a larger share of prosperity for the people or for oneself. Quite the contrary; we should always labor to ameliorate or to do away with misery wherever it may be found. But it is condemnable and sinful to seek, under pretext of making every one happy, to despoil those who have property justly acquired for the benefit of others who have no title to it. Men talk of "equality," but if all the wealth of the world were divided equally amongst all men, this grand "equality," in spite of every law, would not last one day, nor, perhaps, one hour. One would be perpetually beginning over again.

But what if the State were to become owner of all property? Then every one would want to be fed, housed, and clothed without doing any work. The result would be unspeakable confusion and frightful tyranny of the strong over the weak.

VIII

Thou shalt not bear false witness against thy neighbor

Personal credit and a good name may be classed as riches; we must defend them in ourselves against unjust aggression and we have no right to attack them in others.

Hence it is a sin to bear false witness before a judge or to accuse some one unjustly; to spread false reports; to impute vices to our neighbor which he has not, or to charge him with bad deeds which he has not committed (which is calumny); to make known without necessity the vices and faults of others (which is detraction); without any serious reason to think evil of others (which is rash judgment); to vilify others in their absence, to revile them; to listen with pleasure to such talk, etc.

Our divine Lord has said: "Judge not, and you shall not be judged. Condemn not, and you shall not be condemned. Forgive, and you shall be forgiven." (St. Luke VI. 37.)

It is also a sin to reveal a secret confided to us; to forge documents or signatures.

Falsehood dishonors him who is guilty of it; sincerity and uprightness on the contrary make us loved by God and man. Furthermore when the falsehood injures any one, it is a species of theft; and consequently the guilty person, as far as he can, is bound to repair the harm which he has done.

To conclude: Never say of others what you would not wish to be said of yourself; never do to others what you would not wish done to yourself.

CHAPTER XXV

THE COMMANDMENTS OF THE CHURCH

ONE day, in Jerusalem, a member of the Sanhedrim approached our Lord and asked Him: "Which is the first Commandment of all?"

And our Lord answered: "The first commandment of all is, *Hear, O Israel: the Lord thy God is one God.*

And thou shalt love the Lord thy God, with thy whole heart, and with thy whole soul, and with thy whole mind, and with thy whole strength. This is the first commandment.

And the second is like to it: *Thou shalt love thy neighbor as thyself.* There is no other commandment greater than these." (S. Mark. XII. 28–32.)

In order that man may realize this ideal and accomplish his destiny, our divine Lord has completed the Decalogue with other commandments; To propagate the Gospel, (S. Matth. XXVIII. 18). To establish the family such as God made it in the beginning, maintaining the indissolubility of the marriage tie (St. Matth. XIX, 6). To re-

ceive Baptism (St. John, III. 5) and to make use
of the other Sacraments which He has instituted
(St. John XX; 22; *ibid*. VI; St. Luke, XV. 3).
To obey the Catholic Church and the laws or
commandments which she proclaims in order to
provide for men of good-will the means of salvation until the end of time. (S. Matth. XVIII.
18; S. John XXI; 15; S. Luke X. 16) and else-
where.

Christ, in fact, as appears from these texts, has
founded His Church in the form of a hierarchical
society, with power "to bind, and to loose," that
is: to make laws; to dispense from them, and to
abrogate them, according to the spiritual needs
of the Faithful, her children. Hence the laws of
the Church are indirectly *divine laws*, for the
Church can only make them by the power and
with the assistance of God. Therefore they are
of obligation, binding on the conscience — except in the case where for a just and grave reason
we may be dispensed from them: "He that
heareth you, heareth me: and he that despiseth
you, despiseth me. And he that despiseth me,
despiseth him that sent me." (S. Luke, X. 16.)

The Church can dispense from the laws which
she herself has made; from fasting, from abstinence from meat on certain days, etc. But she
cannot, obviously, dispense from any Commandment of God.

As all legislators do, the Church has established penalties for her children who rebel against her laws. They are: *Suspension* by which an ecclesiastic is prevented from exercising his functions; *Interdict* which "interdicts" the use of the Sacraments and Christian burial; *Excommunication* by which the guilty person is cut off from the Church.

To remove these penalties or censures, the Confessor must have special powers from his Bishop or from the Pope himself.

There are six principal Commandments of the Church which are of obligation for the generality of the Faithful.

There are in addition many others which concern either the Clergy, or Religious, or the Faithful in certain isolated actions of the Christian life; the prohibition against joining condemned secret Societies, such as Freemasonry, the prohibition of books, reviews or newspapers contrary to faith or morals.

The Six principal Commandments of the Church are:

1. To hear Mass on Sundays and all holidays of obligation.

2. To fast and abstain on the days commanded.

3. To confess our sins at least once a year.

4. To receive *worthily* the Blessed Eucharist at Easter, or within the time appointed.

5. To contribute to the support of our pastors.

6. Not to solemnize marriage at the forbidden times — nor to marry persons within the forbidden degrees of kindred — nor otherwise prohibited by the Church — nor clandestinely.

I

TO HEAR MASS ON ALL SUNDAYS AND HOLIDAYS
OF OBLIGATION

We are commanded by this first Commandment of the Church to keep the feasts commanded, or of obligation, in the same manner as Sunday; these are: the Feast of the Nativity or Christmas Day; of the Circumcision or New Year's Day, of the Epiphany or Twelfth Day; the Ascension, the Assumption, All Saints; in Ireland, the Feast of St. Patrick and, in many countries, the Feast of St. Joseph is now observed as a holiday of obligation. On these feasts we are obliged under pain of sin to abstain from all heavy manual labor, and to assist at Mass. Pious Catholics will also receive Holy Communion.

On Christmas Day we celebrate the Birth of our divine Savior Who according to tradition was born at midnight on the 25th December in Bethlehem.

On the Feast of the Circumcision we celebrate the Presentation of our Divine Lord in the Temple.

On the Epiphany or Twelfth Day we celebrate
the Adoration of the Divine Child by the Magi.

On Ascension Thursday our Lord ascended into
Heaven, forty days after He had risen again.

The Feast of the Assumption (15th August) is
the day on which according to the tradition of the
Church our Lady after her death was assumed
into Heaven by angels.

On All Saints Day (1st Nov.) we honor all the
blessed souls who are enjoying the Beatific
Vision.

Besides these feasts of obligation, there are
others called feasts of devotion, established in
honor of our Lord, of our Lady, of the Angels,
and of the Saints. Pious Catholics may observe
them all, if they wish, but there is no obligation
to do so.

This applies also to Rogation days (the word,
Rogation means prayers); the exercises of
"the Month of Mary" (May); retreats and
missions.

Why these feasts? The Jewish people observed
festivals, some of them appointed by God Himself,
in commemoration of the great events of their
history; the Catholic Church has acted similarly.
Throughout the course of the year she wishes to
associate all who belong to her with the marvelous events of her past history, and at the same
time, amid the dark night of this world, she il-

lumines with a more intense light the future towards which we are making our way. Thus the feasts are as beacon-fires to guide us on our road to eternity.

—————

God wishes that each week we should consecrate to Him one day of rest and prayer. This day in the Old Law was the Sabbath Day, or Saturday. On that day the Jews assembled in the Temple of Jerusalem or in their synagogues where they listened to the reading, with comments, of the Sacred Books, and prayed. Their principal act of worship was always the offering of sacrifice in the Temple; the immolation of a domestic animal — as for instance a lamb — offered by the priest as a mark of homage rendered to the Supreme God.

The Church continues the office of the Synagogue. But, the Mediator expected by the Synagogue having come, and having replaced all their sacrifices by the sacrifice of Himself, it is around Him that the Church assembles the Faithful on her day of prayer, which is now Sunday — the day on which our Lord rose from the dead.

The sanctification of this day is of obligation. Therefore if a Catholic who has attained the use of reason, fails through his own fault and without sufficient cause to hear Mass on Sunday, he commits a grave sin.

We must assist at the whole Mass from the beginning to the end, respectfully, attentively, devoutly; we may say the prayers for Mass as given in the Prayer books, or the Rosary or any other prayers we wish; or meditate; or join in public prayers or singing.

If a person is ill or nursing the sick, if people live at too great a distance from the Church, or in a word, if they are prevented by any serious cause from hearing Mass, they should at least abstain from servile work on these days.

II

TO FAST AND ABSTAIN ON THE DAYS COMMANDED

Lent consists of 40 fast days which precede the Festival of Easter and begin on Ash Wednesday. On each of these forty days with the exception of Sundays we are bound to fast.

Those who fast can take only one full meal in the day, but they are allowed to take another lighter meal at some hour determined by local custom, and (again) liquid refreshment, not of a notably nourishing character, to which however, an ounce of solid food may on one occasion be added.

During Lent we fast as a penance for our sins, to prepare our hearts for our Easter Communion, and following the example of our divine Lord who before preaching the Gospel fasted during forty days.

The term Quarter Tense is applied to the Wednesday, Friday and Saturday which come at four recurring seasons of the year.

The word Vigil signifies the *eve* or day before a Feast.

On certain fast days the use of meat is forbidden; on all other fast days the use of meat is allowed at the principal meal.

All who are under twenty-one years of age and those persons who are in their sixtieth year are exempt from the law of fasting, as are also the sick, and all who are engaged in exhausting occupations.

We abstain from meat on Friday because on that day our Lord died for us, and because the Church wishes us to practise every week some penance in expiation for our sins in union with our divine Savior.

People say to us: "Meat is as good on Friday as on another day." Obviously. We are not forbidden to eat it because it is bad, but because it is a question of imposing on ourselves a slight mortification, which is moreover excellent from the point of view of hygiene.

III

TO CONFESS OUR SINS AT LEAST ONCE A YEAR

The early Christians were very frequent communicants and fervent in severe and public penitential exercises. During succeeding ages, however, this devout spirit gradually grew weaker. Therefore the Church ordained that the Faithful should approach the Sacraments of Penance and the Blessed Eucharist at least once a year. (Gen. Lateran Council, XIII. century.)

The natural time for an annual confession is of course at Easter, when we are also obliged to receive Holy Communion. We must confess all our grievous sins and repent of them sincerely. A bad confession would not satisfy our obligation; such a confession would only add the crime of sacrilege to our sins and render us more guilty.

A good Catholic will not be satisfied with going to confession once a year. If a man should commit mortal sin, he acts very wrongly and foolishly if he keep it on his conscience. If he fall ill, if he be in imminent danger of committing sin, if he be about to undertake a long or dangerous journey, he ought to go to confession that he may be preserved in a state of grace. If we cannot go at once to confession, we should as soon as possible seek to recover God's favor by making an Act of perfect contrition (see under "Penance"); such an act at once restores us to the state of grace. Death comes as a thief in the night at the moment when we least expect it: therefore is it folly to risk remaining in mortal sin. For this reason pious Catholics approach the Sacraments on all the great feasts of the year; numbers do so every month, others every week, whilst many are daily communicants. Such as these are always prepared to appear before God.

The practise of Confession equally with the observance of all the Commandments of the Church has a priceless value for society as well as for the individual. By it, in truth, the Church strives to secure for all her members moral perfection. By it she secures reparation of injustices and restitution of rights. And if throughout the entire world, all those who by Baptism have become Christians, high and low, rich and poor, rulers and ruled, were to go to Confession regularly and with the requisite dispositions, how magnificent human society would become! How we should emulate one another in virtue. How many crimes, scandals, lawsuits, wars, revolutions, and other calamities would be averted!

IV

TO RECEIVE HOLY COMMUNION AT EASTER OR THEREABOUTS

This Commandment is of obligation for all Catholics as soon as they reach the years of discretion and are sufficiently instructed in the truths of religion.

Is it not wonderful that Our divine Lord not only permits us to receive Him in Holy Communion, but actually commands us to do so? "Unless you eat my flesh and drink my blood," He says, "you shall not have life in you." Let us merely remark that those who make sacrilegious Communions do not obey this Commandment; on the contrary, to their other sins they add a fearful crime.

The obligation of Confession and Communion at least once a year is a serious one; those who neglect it wilfully disobey God and the Church; they grow hardened in sin; they scandalize the faithful; by refusing to respond to the call of Jesus Christ, they treat Him with contempt.

If at Easter we should be ill, then we should make this known to the priest and receive Holy Communion at home. Finally if we are unable to discharge this duty at the prescribed time, or have wilfully neglected it, we are obliged to fulfil the obligation as soon as possible.

Such is the Commandment. But a pious Catholic will receive Holy Communion frequently that he may conquer Satan, correct his bad habits, keep away temptation, obtain God's grace, preserve and increase within him supernatural life, and thus more surely save his soul.

Further those who are in danger of death should not only go to Confession, but should also receive Holy Communion that they may be strengthened for the dreadful passage from time to eternity.

V

TO CONTRIBUTE TO THE SUPPORT OF OUR PASTORS

The inhabitants of a State recognize without any arguments that they are bound in proportion to their means to bear their share in the public expenditure by regular contributions. Of necessity all Catholics are under a similar obligation in what concerns the expenses incurred for the fitting celebration of divine Worship, and for all works connected with it. Each one according to his means is bound to afford the Catholic Church material assistance, to enable her to exercise her functions, to maintain her position and to develop: this should be for all Catholics worthy of the name an honor and a privilege which they will not willingly forego.

VI

NOT TO SOLEMNIZE MARRIAGE AT THE FORBIDDEN
TIMES, NOR TO MARRY PERSONS WITHIN THE
FORBIDDEN DEGREES OF KINDRED, NOR
OTHERWISE PROHIBITED BY THE CHURCH, NOR
CLANDESTINELY. (See Chapter on Matrimony.)

CHAPTER XXVI

THE EVANGELICAL COUNSELS

Religious Life

A YOUNG man approaching our divine Lord, said to Him: "Master, what shall I do that I may have life everlasting?" And Jesus answered: "If thou wilt enter into life, keep the Commandments." "What are they?" inquired the young man. Jesus answered: "Thou shalt do no murder. Thou shalt not commit adultery, Thou shalt not steal, Thou shalt not bear false witness, Honor thy father and thy mother; and, Thou shalt love thy neighbor as thyself. The young man saith to him: All these have I kept from my youth, what is yet wanting to me? Jesus saith to him: If thou wilt be perfect, go sell what thou hast, and give to the poor, and thou shalt have treasure in heaven: and come, follow me. And when the young man had heard this word, he went away sad; for he had great possessions. . . ."

Then Peter said to him: "Behold we have left all things, and have followed thee: what therefore shall we have?"

And Jesus said to them: "Amen I say to you, that you, who have followed me, in the regeneration, when the son of man shall sit on the seat of his majesty, you also shall sit on twelve seats judging the twelve tribes of Israel.

And every one that hath left house, or brethren, or sisters, or father, or mother, or wife, or children, or lands for my name's sake: shall receive an hundred fold, and shall possess life everlasting." (Matth. XIX. 16–29.)"

Since this page of the Gospel was written, how many young men, how many young girls anxious about this same matter have approached the divine Master, saying: "What shall I do with my life, so as to employ it best in the interests of God, of souls, of my own interests, that I may not spend my time on earth uselessly, and that I may surely gain Heaven?"

And the divine Master's answer, soft and low yet decided, has ever been the same: "If in addition to the faithful observance of the Commandments, you seek for greater perfection, come and follow Me."

The Evangelical Counsels indeed have been given as an ideal to be aimed at — the ideal of Christian Perfection. "In Religious Congregations," said Guizot, "concentrated Christianity has reached its highest degree."

There have always been souls athirst for self-sacrifice; desirous of consecrating themselves wholly to the service of God and of their neighbor; eager for every sacrifice. From the beginning of the Christian Era we find virgins and widows assisting the Apostles and their successors.

Later the deserts of Palestine and of Egypt were peopled with solitaries. Later still St. Basil in the East, St. Augustine at Hippo, St. Benedict in the West, organized the religious life, properly so called. In the Middle Ages and the following centuries, St. Francis of Assisi, St. Dominic, St. Clare, St. Teresa, and St. Ignatius of Loyola founded new orders, and continually up to the present day other congregations or associations have sprung up to meet the wants of society, of the Church and of souls.

It is necessary in fact that outside the parochial clergy and ordinary Christians there should be bands of volunteers who can devote themselves to special works, and thus supply certain social and religious needs; who will pray and do penance, and when the divine anger is excited by the sins of men, will serve as lightning conductors; who will by their example, by teaching, by preaching, preserve or revive Christian life; who will instruct children, nurse the sick, evangelize the heathen, and extend ever more and more the boundaries of true civilization.

The Apostle, St. John, points out three great passions or concupiscences which are opposed to Christian perfection: an inordinate desire for the things of this world, pride, and sensuality. To these three causes of imperfection, of sin, of eternal ruin, the Church by the counsel of her divine Master opposes Voluntary Poverty, Chastity, and Obedience, which may be the subject of vows, public or private, temporary or perpetual, simple or solemn, practised in Religious Life or outside it.

Voluntary Poverty consists in the renunciation of all right of possession (the vow of Poverty is thus understood in the Religious Orders the members of which take solemn vows), or at least the right of disposing freely of one's property without the permission of Superiors (as in Congregations in which simple vows are taken).

The vow of Chastity binds to celibacy, and by a new and special obligation forbids every act opposed to chastity.

The vow of Obedience imposes the obligation of obeying a lawful Superior in matters connected with the observance of the Rule.

Is it necessary to answer here the objection which has sometimes been urged that "the rights given by Nature should not be renounced?"

There are indeed certain essential rights which

with their correlative duties we are not permitted to renounce. But there are many secondary natural rights the use of which are by no means of obligation, such as the right of possession, the right to get married, the right to submit oneself to a Superior, the right to live in solitude or in community, the right to wear such or such a costume, etcetera.

These rights also constitute liberties. And if they are renounced in order to make use of other rights of a superior nature, such as to devote one's life to the service of one's neighbor, obviously one attains to a higher degree in the scale of moral perfection. To maintain otherwise would be to place egotism above all self-sacrifice.

In offering to God for His service and the service of his brethren, the sacrifice of his goods, his body, and his will the Religious gives all that he has, and enters upon a new state — the state of aiming at perfection. Thus bound to God, he can no longer withdraw unless for grave reasons and on condition that he is released from his vows by a special act of his Superiors or of the Pope himself.

For this reason the religious state must not be embraced lightly. But those who are called to it by a real vocation — consisting of real aptitude, of a pure intention, of acceptance by a Religious superior and with the advice of a wise

director — such would do well — although not
strictly obliged in conscience to do so — to respond
to this call; if they are free to dispose of their
persons no authority has any right to oppose
them. No authority, in fact, unless it is abused,
can hinder a Christian who, following the counsels
of Jesus Christ, wishes to serve God more faithfully, to devote himself more completely to the
service of his brethren and the salvation of his
own soul.

Entrance into the religious state is always preceded by a noviciate, during which no engagements
can be contracted. Subjects are only received on
condition that they are not necessary, morally or
materially, to their parents, and that they are
themselves free from all natural encumbrance or
obligation.

CHAPTER XXVII

CIVIL LAWS

Society — The State — The Citizen

WITHOUT order it is impossible for Society to exist; for the preservation of its existence regulations are necessary, authority is necessary, a guiding power is necessary: all of which is implied in Order.

Now it being necessary, in order that certain advantages may be common to all, that Society should exist, the directing power which maintains these conditions of its existence, having regard to our natural and supernatural ends, must partake of both the divine and natural order. And it is in this sense that St. Paul says: "For there is no power but of God" (Rom. XIII. 1).

But ordinarily God does not interfere in the choosing of the leaders of the people; — He did so in the case of the Jewish people — conformably to the general designs of His Providence in all these matters He permits men to use their free will, and to submit themselves to whatever government they prefer, which in general is that which they merit.

The first elements of Society consisted of the first families, and the first one of these families was that which came directly from the hands of the Creator; so that, speaking historically and rationally, we find God at the beginning of everything. "Society," says Cicero, "was formed in the first instance by the union of husband and wife, then by that of children with their parents, afterwards a whole household became the first element of a city, and as it were the germ of a republic."

Civil Society therefore is not an association of individuals, but an association of families. On this fundamental principle must be based all good legislation, which should place the interests of the public before those of private persons.

The government in civil Society comprises the legislative power which formulates the laws; the executive power which regulates these and sees that they are executed; the judicial government which passes judgment on crimes, misdemeanors and disputes according to the laws in force.

Thus the government or the State has all the means necessary for the exercise of its special functions with the right to legislate; to have the laws carried into execution; to impose obedience to these laws as a matter of conscience, and if necessary to punish even with death those who contravene them.

In all this the aim of the government should be to provide for the common welfare, not only by protecting individual right, by suppressing disturbances, by defending the country against enemy aggression; but also by endeavoring to afford the people the means of acquiring honestly the largest amount possible of material, intellectual, and moral good. It will do this not only by the laws and regulations which it may ordain, but also and above all by encouraging private action, and by seconding all the good measures initiated by individuals or particular associations.

But the State does not possess unlimited power. Whatever may be the form of government, — autocratic, constitutional, democratic, the principle of supreme power resides neither in a man, nor in a delegation, nor in a people. "Ten thousand ignorant men would not make one man of knowledge," says Benjamin Constant. "The will of a whole people could not make what is unjust just." (Taine.) And "The approval of millions could not make truth of error." (Clemenceau.)

In the exercise of government men are the delegates of God. They have therefore as their first duty to comply with the divine will as manifested in the moral law which is engraved on man's conscience or written in the Decalogue.

All legislation which violates this law is unlawful and tyrannical, and is against the interests of society itself. Further, in presence of revealed religion the State cannot treat it with indifference; respect and protection are due to it.

Within these limits the State has all the powers necessary for the government of the nation. It ought to repress all grave abuse of individual liberty injurious to the liberty of other citizens. It ought to protect public morality, for moral depravity is fatal to the family and to society. It has power to levy taxes to the extent necessary for the payment of public charges. It ought to establish the schools which are indispensable for the education of youth, but never forgetting that in this it is only acting in virtue of a commission from the parents themselves. Finally the State will regard it as a duty not only to respect but to promote everywhere within its administration the fundamental virtues of honesty, of justice, of self-respect, of honor, courage and patriotism. And the more these virtues rest upon God, the more solid they will be; the more surely they will render society strong and prosperous.

To enable individuals, families, and society to fulfil their destiny and to attain their respective ends, nothing is equal to religion and nothing can take its place. No doubt the various religions differ in form and in their main points, according as they are nearer or further removed from truth. But they always have some connection with it, even in their simplest expressions, by a certain number of essential ideas, such as respect for a supreme Power, the reality of an invisible world, the necessity of worship, certain moral obligations, the organization of the family. And it is because of this that so many heathen tribes and nations both of antiquity and at the present day have been able to exist and to develop.

Hence Plutarch echoing Plato wrote, "It would be easier to build a town in the air than to form and maintain a city without religion." Now if these imperfect religions have the effect of a cement, as it were, in consolidating the whole social edifice, what would be the efficacy of the Christian Religion in a country where it was really recognized and practised as it should be, integrally and universally? No doubt this is an ideal, but an ideal which is obligatory, and which should serve as a constant guide to the efforts of the governing powers and of those governed.

From these considerations we must not conclude that the State is asked to become a theocracy. "Render to Cæsar," says our divine Lord, "what belongs to Cæsar, and to God what belongs to God." By these words a radical distinction is drawn between the two governments, the civil and the religious, which pagan civilization had joined and confounded. But this distinction by no means implies separation, indifference, or still less hostility. If Cæsar is ridiculous when he claims to press God into his service, he is hateful when in the abused name of free thought he treats Him as a disturber, a suspect, a stranger.

Therefore it is as natural as it is desirable that there should be union and harmony between the two Societies, civil and religious. This union permits of the independence of the State in purely civil matters, of the independence of the Church in purely religious matters, and of agreement on mixed matters. It can therefore be perfectly reconciled in practise with all legitimate liberties. The Church is never opposed to these, but only to irreligious and immoral tendencies which are too often concealed under magnificent and alluring appearances and names.

With these considerations in view, it is easy for the Catholic to know his rights and his duties with regard to the civil society of which he forms part. His rights and his duties are indeed those of all citizens. But he who recognizes God as the Author of Society, the first principle of Authority, and the necessary basis of Moral Law, will therefore bring to the exercise of his civic activities dispositions of a nature at once more profound and more elevated.

In the first place, he will have a correct idea of

what the State is. The State must not be confounded with Society, nor can it be compared to the father of a family who is charged by nature with the providing for the welfare of his children, feeding them, instructing them, settling them in life; nor to a sovereign lord who can and should regulate everything, order everything, direct everything.

The function of the State is simply to organize the public services as well as possible in the interests of the country; to insure safety, order, liberty; to suppress vice, crime and misdemeanors prejudicial to the community; to prescribe the practise of some indispensable moral virtues, to secure a certain amount of temporal goods. It is the duty of each individual to take the initiative towards the full development of his faculties and to the promotion of his own interests within the limits of the law and the higher ordinances of morality.

The true believer will not rest satisfied with merely gaining a livelihood and allowing himself to be governed. But as far as his intelligence and position in life permit him, he will wish to give active help in relieving want and misery, in doing good in every way, in stimulating progress in every calling, and in furthering the prosperity of the country to its fullest extent. If he has the right to vote, this right constitutes for him a duty—the duty of voting rightly, intelligently and conscientiously. By his uprightness, his honesty, his diligence, his kindness, he will gain for the faith which inspires him love and respect.

The religion which he practises in his daily life does indeed penetrate to the innermost recesses of conscience. It forbids to those in whom authority is vested all abuse of that authority, such as manifesting partiality, and all vexatious proceedings against those over whom they are placed, whilst at the same time it prescribes to subjects obedience to just laws, respect for the legitimate government, devotion to public affairs, resistance to anarchy. This religion combats vice in every form, selfishness, immorality, drunkenness, fraud, exploitation of the poor, of women, of children; it patronizes literature, science and art; it relieves distress; it improves morals; it inspires the unfortunate with hope; it ennobles souls; draws all ranks nearer to one another; calms angry passions, and tends to the maintenance everywhere of order; that order which is based on justice and charity.

Thus the good Catholic — he who understands his Faith and lives according to it, is necessarily a good citizen, loyal and devoted. His country for him is not merely the earth which feeds him but the whole of those material, intellectual, moral and religious blessings in which he shares;

it is an extension of his family, of his house, of his substance; it is the guardian of the hearths, the cradles, the tombs and the altars of the community. The joys and the glory of our country are ours; as are ours also her labors, her trials, and her sufferings. The Catholic cannot be indifferent to her lot. In the chain of generations of which he is a link, it is his pride and consolation not to cause a break; the supernatural life which animated his forefathers abounds in him also. To acquire honor, it is not necessary that his family should have written their name in history; it is enough if they have given to their country an uninterrupted succession of toilers and defenders, upright citizens and good Christians. In him is continued the succession. The earth which he treads under foot is composed of their dust, and he draws his life from it. A modest yet healthy tree in the great national forest, he has come at the time and to the place allotted to him; he has had his share of the circumambient light and shade; he has expanded in the sun and trembled in the tempest. When he falls others will carry on in their turn. In transmitting to them the torch of truth which he received from his forefathers in the far-off past, he will close his eyes only to open them again in the same instant to the eternal light in which he shall meet again those who have gone before him.

And there he will wait for those who shall follow him until the last general meeting at which all the elect of the human race shall assemble.

In dying, the Catholic can console himself with the reflection that he has understood the meaning of life.

CHAPTER XXVIII

Religion and Its External Practises

WORSHIP in its most general sense is homage rendered to a person or thing. As far back as we can go in the history of the human race, we find worship positively asserting itself as the exterior expression of all religion, at the same time as dogma and morals on which it rests. Prayers in public and in private, gestures of supplication, of veneration, of adoration, of repentance, of expiation; offerings, libations, sacrifices, confession of faults committed, with the intention of obtaining their remission, varied ordinances, symbols, and formulas, consecrated objects and places, special ministers, religious feasts and assemblies, all that totality of exterior manifestations: this is found everywhere, ever and always from the beginning, more or less well organized amongst the most civilized nations, as in the midst of the most primitive tribes. It is common capital belonging to the whole human race and resting on the universal belief that our external world in which we are living at present is dominated by an invisible world into which through the gate of death we shall ourselves enter.

These beliefs and these practises in their essentials form part of the organization of the family and thence they extend to the tribe; they maintain it; they defend it; they insure its permanence and its development.

Without religion and worship, the family would disappear; with religion and its worship which gives to it an ideal, a moral law and discipline, the family becomes a tribe, and the tribe becomes a nation. Thus it is that the constitution of powerful nations, such as Egypt, Greece, the Roman Republic, Persia, China, Japan, etc. became possible. The fundamental and necessary bases of all social organization are religion and the Family.

Thus has it been from the beginning. Unfortunately as the sons of Adam dispersed through the world, they forgot, distorted, and overloaded the pure primitive ideas which had been given to them. By degrees their worship without wholly losing sight of God was addressed particularly to the *manes* of the dead, to spirits, to the forces of Nature, to those various divinities of which pagan mythology is full. Hence superstition and magic were substituted for religion, giving rise to the paganism of the fetish-worshipers of Africa, of Oceanica, of America, as well as to the ancient religious forms of Egypt, Assyria, of Greece and of Rome, as well as to those which still prevail in Northern India, China and Japan.

But at the same time some of the sons of Adam remained faithful to God and to His worship. And thus it is that in the Bible we find the first heads of families represented as offering to the Author of the world sacrifices usually accompanied with prayers, ceremonies and external rites. This worship of the patriarchs is like a slender current of pure water in the middle of a stream which grows wider as it advances through the ages, and the banks of which become more and more encumbered with strange commodities.

Then came Moses, the law-giver to the Jewish people, whose mission it was to codify the primitive worship and that of the patriarchs, to organize and complete it, keeping in view the expected supreme Law-giver, the Messias.

The object of the Mosaic Worship is God, the only living personal all-powerful God, the Creator and Lord of all, Who alone is adorable, Who cannot be represented, and Whose very Name is mysterious. This Name is written with four consonants, J. H. V. H. and is pronounced something like "Jahveh," a word from which "Jehovah" has been formed.

The essence of this worship was sacrifice, and a bloody sacrifice, that is the immolation of a victim — a lamb, for example — offered to God in acknowledgment of His supreme dominion over Nature, in honor of His sovereign Majesty, and to redeem life with a life. The partaking of the victim sacrificed was the symbol of reconciliation. There were also private and public offerings and libations.

One day of the week — the seventh — was consecrated to worship; this was the Sabbath or day of rest. The people assembled on certain great feasts which recalled to them the principal events of their marvelous history: the Feast of the Pasch in remembrance of the Exodus from Egypt; the Feast of Pentecost in remembrance of the proclamation of the Law on Mount Sinai; the Feast of Tabernacles or of Tents in remembrance of their wandering in the desert; the Feast of Atonement or "Kippour" in atonement for the sins of the people.

For a long time the place of worship was a "tabernacle," that is a large tent with an enclosed space in front of it. Within this tent was a reserved portion called the "Holy of holies" which contained the Tables of the Law enclosed in the Ark of the Covenant. Later a magnificent temple was built on the same plan by Solomon at Jerusalem.

By degrees other places of worship called synagogues or assemblies were opened, in which the Jews assembled under the presidency of the "Head of the Synagogue." The office began with prayer, then followed the reading of the Law and the Prophets with a sermon, after which a blessing brought the ceremony to an end.

The priesthood was the exclusive right of the Tribe of Levi and of the family of Aaron who was the first high priest.

Finally at the time appointed by God and foretold by the Prophets, Jesus Christ appeared on earth. He did not come to destroy the Mosaic or patriarchal worship in its doctrinal or moral part but to complete it, not by a sudden change but by a progressive adaptation with which the Church was charged.

And thus it is that in our Religion everything, worship, dogma, moral law, is traced back through Jesus Christ to Moses, and through Moses to the most ancient representatives of the human race. From our beginning to our end religion binds us to God.

Like the Mosaic Worship and the worship of the Patriarchs, Catholic worship has for its final object God and God alone. For God alone is the Master, the Savior, and the Author of all good. But further, above all, we adore Him, serve Him, and love Him as our Father. He is the "God of Abraham, of Isaac and of Jacob," but He is also the God of the whole world; He is above all the God of those in whom His grace, that is, His life, shines forth brightly. He is the One and Only God, but the Unity of His Essence includes the Trinity of Persons.

The Messias is no longer to come; He has come. He has dwelt amongst us. He has communicated to us that which He had to tell us. And whilst by the Spirit of Truth He directs us invisibly, He dwells Himself in the "Tabernacle" of our temples, and in them daily substitutes the offering of Himself upon the altar for the ancient sacrifices.

God— the Father— the Son— and the Holy Ghost— Jesus Christ made Man: such is the object of Catholic Worship. If we honor the Angels and the Saints— we never adore them — it is with reference to God Who has distinguished them by special graces; Who has given them to us as models, and Who is more affected by their prayer than by ours. Weak and sinful as we are, to obtain more readily a hearing from God we address ourselves to creatures who are better than we are and more powerful. What can be more reasonable?

It is with these sentiments that the Catholic Church has ever rendered special worship to the Blessed Virgin Mary. Since she is the mother

CHAPTER XXIX

THE SACRAMENTS

The Sources of Supernatural Life

EVERY child born into the world, is with regard to Faith in a state of sin, and has forfeited all its rights; it is endowed with the necessary natural faculties, but is deprived of sanctifying grace, and incapable of itself of attaining union with God and eternal happiness.

Of course God could, in a general way, grant this sanctifying grace or supernatural life without the medium of any special rite. He has done so, and no doubt does so still, for many souls who have been prevented by circumstances from having recourse to the Sacraments. Yet in His relations with man it is in accordance with His divine Providence that He should take man as He is. And as we are not pure spirits, spiritual or divine things are communicated to our senses by external signs or symbols: thus for example, the purity of the grace given in Baptism is symbolized by the water which is poured on the head while the sacramental words are being pronounced.

This is the reason why, from the beginning of the human race, we find that in the essentials common to all religions to which allusion was made in the preceding chapter, symbolic rites have been employed as signs — for instance, of spiritual regeneration, of purification, of atonement. Such are the usual family observances by which the chief events of life are marked — birth, coming of age, marriage, death: such are the various religious practises — circumcision, tatooing, aspersions, fumigations, incensing, offerings, feasts; which are to be condemned only in so far as the intention inspiring them and the object to which they apply are to be condemned. These rites were used in the religion of the Patriarchs, and they were codified in the Mosaic Law. And finally our divine Lord sanctified this universal tendency by the institution of the Sacraments and by the power which He has left to the Catholic Church of surrounding them with appropriate ceremonials; with this essential difference that the Sacraments actually give those things of which they are the signs.[1]

Baptism, the first of the Sacraments, raises those who receive it from the state of original sin

[1] The word *Sacrament* comes from the Latin *sacramentum*, something consecrated by invocation to the Divinity, holy, mysterious.

resulting from the fall of our first parents;
purifies their souls from every stain of sin; restores them to the state of grace, and unites them
to that great society which on earth, in purgatory
and in heaven forms the Communion of Saints.

Another of the Sacraments, Confirmation,
strengthens these souls in faith and in the practise of faith.

Another, Holy Eucharist, renders them, so to
speak, divine, by feeding them mysteriously on
the Body and Blood of Jesus Christ. If Christians afterwards by one or more grave sins should
lose this supernatural life, they can regain it in
the Sacrament of Penance.

And when they are in danger of death the Sacrament of Extreme Unction completes the purification of their souls, and fortifies them for the last
supreme struggle of life by preparing them to
appear before their Judge.

As there must be ministers of God to recall
to the people His truths and to insure His worship,
these ministers receive their ordination and
consecration in the Sacrament of Holy Orders.

Finally, the Sacrament of Matrimony unites,
preserves and sanctifies the Christian family by
which the children of God are multiplied on
earth and Heaven is filled with His Elect.

Thus the Catholic Church disposes the seven
Sacraments, which are as so many mysterious

channels by which the supernatural life of grace reaches the human soul, to animate it, to enlighten, adorn and render it worthy of God — of God Who makes of this soul His dwelling place.

Each of these Sacraments allows of an exterior rite, that is, of an outward sign, of ceremonies, of certain words, etc. producing, not assuredly of itself, but by the will of Jesus Christ, the particular kind of interior grace for which it was instituted. For this reason a Sacrament is defined as: "a visible, that is, an outward sign or action, instituted by Christ to give grace."

But in order to participate in the effects of the Sacraments, no obstacle must be placed to them by bad dispositions — to do so would be to profane the Sacraments, to commit sacrilege. For God Who ever has regard to man's free will, gives His divine grace only to those who desire it sincerely.

CHAPTER XXX

BAPTISM — CONFIRMATION — HOLY ORDERS

THERE are three Sacraments which imprint upon the human soul a special and indelible mark or character, for which reason they can only be received once. These Sacraments are Baptism, Confirmation, and Holy Orders: we are baptized, confirmed, ordained, for all eternity, all our infidelities, even apostacy and damnation notwithstanding.

When by Baptism [1] the Church incorporates a human being with herself, she does so forever; even if this human being should deny her, she is ready to receive him once more, provided that he returns to her in all sincerity. He bears her mark, the mark of "regeneration," and in this same life we are not born again.

This applies to Confirmation [2] also.

By this Sacrament the Church assures to those

---

[1] *Baptism*, from the Greek βαπτισμός, washing or purification. The water poured on the head while at the same time are pronounced the words: "I baptize thee, in the name of the Father, and of the Son, and of the Holy Ghost," is the outward sign of Baptism.

[2] From the Greek χρῖσμα.

who have been baptized their rights — which are
at the same time duties — as Catholic citizens and
as soldiers of Jesus Christ.

It is the same with the Sacrament of Holy
Orders.[1] The Church selects certain Christians
and consecrates them as her ministers in the
order of sub-deacons, priests and bishops. This
consecration is irrevocable.

I. BAPTISM

Baptism is the first and the most necessary of
all the Sacraments; without it we should remain
in the state of original sin, deprived of the supernatural life of grace, and as dead in the eyes of
God. It is therefore of the greatest importance
that parents should have their children baptized
as soon as possible after coming into this world,
and so procure for them the priceless benefit of
being born again — born to supernatural life.
This baptismal regeneration is necessary for the
supernaturalization of the child, and, in the
event of its dying before attaining the full use of
reason, for its admittance into the Heaven of
the Elect.

By Baptism all trace of original or actual sin
is effaced; the supernatural life of grace illumines
and adorns the soul; a new Christian enters the
Catholic Church; one more human being is

[1] That is to say: *state, class, rank, condition.*

marked with the sign of God. Further by Baptism a sort of treaty of alliance, an agreement, a contract is established between God and man.

Of himself if an adult, or if an infant through his godfather and godmother, the one baptized renounces Satan and his works—that is to say, sin, indifference, and false religions, and promises to be always faithful to Jesus Christ, to His Religion and to His Law. This is what is called the baptismal vows which are generally renewed when children attain the use of reason. And by the voice of the Church God promises the newly baptized to be faithful to him on His part, to grant him His grace here on earth, and after death to admit him into the glory of Eternity.

A name is given to the newly baptized, usually that of a Saint who will be his patron or protector before God. A godfather and godmother who are, as it were, his spiritual parents, become responsible for him, and in the event of his being deprived by death of his parents, it will become their duty to see that their godchild is instructed in the Catholic Religion in which he has been baptized. It is necessary therefore that these godparents should themselves be Catholics; heretics, excommunicated persons, members of secret societies, public sinners, cannot be accepted as such. Further godparents contract with the child and his parents a spiritual relationship which constitutes an impediment to marriage. Thus the father or mother of the child could not fill this office in his regard. Finally let us add that for a boy a godfather, for a girl a godmother — suffices, as at Confirmation.

The water used in Baptism is blessed in a particular way by the priest at Easter or Pentecost. But if this water, called "baptismal water," is not at hand, ordinary natural water may be used. Baptism is administered by pouring the water on the head; if this cannot be done and there is urgency, the water can be poured over any other part of the body. To the priest belongs the right of giving baptism, but in case of necessity any one may and ought to give baptism. They will administer it by pouring the water on the child's forehead, at the same time pronouncing distinctly the following words: "N—— I baptise thee, in the name of the Father, and of the Son, and of the Holy Ghost." This is called "private baptism," that is, baptism without the usual ceremonies, which are supplied, if possible later on by a priest. Private baptism is valid, but only in case of necessity should people have recourse to it.

If an infidel in danger of death and sufficiently instructed sincerely desires to be baptized and repents of his sins, this desire, being what is called *Baptism of desire*, will suffice to obtain for him a death in the state of grace and entrance into Heaven; but faith, repentance, and the love of God must accompany this desire, which is in reality an act of perfect charity. It is not even necessary that this desire should be explicitly expressed. But should this infidel recover from his illness, he must take care to receive baptism of water as soon as possible.

With still greater reason does he, who, whilst not yet baptized but desirous of it, suffers death rather than deny Jesus Christ or the Catholic Religion, receive complete pardon of his sins and go straight to Heaven, having received the baptism of blood (St. Matth. XVI, 25).

The symbolism of Baptism is not new; lustrations and purification by water as in the baptism of our Lord by John the Baptist have been observed in all ages.

In almost every nation the birth of a child is accompanied or followed by similar ceremonies, during which a name is given to the newly-born. The Jews from the time of Abraham observed the rite of circumcision, by which the child was made one of the people of God. What is new in Christian Baptism is the efficacy which is joined to the rite, as we know from the express declaration of our Lord; this efficacy, which produces "regeneration by water and the word," differentiates it radically from all other anterior types, which were moreover a figure of it and a preparation for it.

The ceremonies which accompany the baptismal ablution are ancient and very characteristic. The child is brought to the church door by the godfather and the godmother, of whom the priest inquires, "What do you ask of the Church of God?" to which they answer "Faith." The priest then, to drive out all influence of the Evil Spirit, exorcises the child, making over it the sign of the Cross, the sign of our Redemption; he then puts a little salt into the child's mouth whilst he prays that God would preserve this soul from the corruption of sin; after which he introduces the child into the church. The godparents, always speaking in the name of the child, now make their profession of faith (by reciting the Creed), renounce Satan and formally ask for baptism. The priest then baptizes the child which is held at the font by the godparents. He next makes a Cross with holy oil (chrism [1] from the Greek Chrisma, oil which has been blest). on the infant's head; invests it with a white garment, and places in its hand a lighted taper symbol of the new life, pure and luminous, into which that child has entered. One more Christian has been born to the Church of God and has taken the first step on the road to eternity.

[1] From the Greek χρῖσμα, consecrated oil used for anointing.

II. CONFIRMATION

Confirmation is a Sacrament which has for its end and effect the giving of special grace from the Holy Ghost and the strengthening of the Faith received in Baptism. It is, so to speak, the complement of that first Sacrament. It brings Christian life to its fullness. It is not indispensable to salvation, but it greatly facilitates it, and not to receive it through indifference or neglect would be a fault.

Usually this Sacrament is given by a bishop, but in exceptional circumstances and by special permission of the Pope it can be administered by a simple priest.

For the administration of Confirmation the Bishop begins by extending his hands over the heads of the candidates, invoking for them the "seven gifts of the Holy Ghost: wisdom, understanding, counsel, fortitude, knowledge, piety and fear of the Lord." Then with the holy chrism (made of oil and balm which is blessed on Holy Thursday) he traces a cross on their foreheads; by this sign the Christian is marked and placed amongst the soldiers of Christ. Finally the Bishop strikes each one lightly on the cheek, to teach him that he must be prepared to suffer everything for his religion and his faith.

As in Baptism, those to be confirmed — if boys,

must have a godfather; if girls, a godmother. The same godfather or godmother can act for a number. But parents cannot fill the office.

Finally the newly-confirmed in public profession of their faith recite the Credo, to which they add the Pater and Ave as the initiation of prayer, these being the ordinary prayers of a Christian.

By Confirmation the children of God are made His soldiers. They are marked indelibly with His sign, and engage to serve Him without human respect bravely and enthusiastically, to render testimony to Him to propagate His religion, to honor Him, and if necessary to suffer and to die for Him.

III. HOLY ORDERS

As from the beginning Religion in some form has always existed, consequently at the same time there has also always been a priesthood, that is to say, ministers of sacred things, "ancients," "elders" or priests. Such was Adam; such were Enoch, Noe, Melchisedech, Abraham, and after them under the Mosaic Law the ministers of Religion — the High-priest, priests and Levites.[1] However, these were but a figure of and a preparation for the Priesthood of the New Law. In the New Law Jesus Christ is the sole Redeemer, the

---

[1] That is: men of the tribe of Levi, from which should be recruited the ministers of the Mosaic Worship.

sole Mediator, the sole Intermediary between Heaven and Earth, and consequently the sole Priest. But according to the general arrangements of His Providence He has willed that certain men should be His earthly and temporary deputies — such are the Catholic bishops and priests. Hence the Sacrament of Holy Orders which consecrates them and gives to them the powers and the graces necessary for the exercise of their sacred functions: to offer the Sacrifice of the adorable Body and Blood of our divine Savior; to remit the sins of men; to dispense supernatural life by means of the Sacraments; to teach the truths of religion; to preside at public worship and to render to the faithful from their birth to their death all the services in the spiritual order which they may need for the sanctification and the salvation of their souls.

On our part we have duties towards our priests: to listen to their instructions; to help them in their ministry; to defend them against calumny; and, as far as our means permit us, to provide for their material wants whilst they themselves are consecrating their lives to insure to us all spiritual blessings.

The word Orders (from the Latin *Ordo*, in the sense of rank, class, social condition) is applied very rightly to the Sacrament by which the hierarchy of the ministers of the Church is created from the minor orders to the sub-deaconship, deaconship, priesthood and episcopate.[1]

Those who receive this Sacrament are the fewer in number. But everywhere God calls whom He wishes — without any merit on their part — to labor for the salvation of their brethren.

This "call of God" is what we term a *Vocation*. Those thus called should respond: God will be faithful to them.

In the Church the Pope or Sovereign Pontiff is as Bishop of Rome the successor of St. Peter, and the first of the Bishops of the whole Church. The Bishops alone like the Apostles constitute the Priesthood in its complete fulness; it is because of this that they alone administer the Sacrament of Holy Orders.

Once a priest, forever a priest; nothing can take away this stamp of priesthood which will remain for all eternity. But to hear confessions, every priest must be approved of for this office, and must receive jurisdiction from the bishop, as every bishop receives jurisdiction from the Pope.[2]

Once consecrated sub-deacon, the priest is bound: 1st to recite daily the devotional exercises

[1] We have seen already that the word, priest (presbyter) signifies — aged man, ancient, a venerable man; in the primitive Church, the priests were always chosen from amongst the elders.

[2] *Juris-diction*, that is the power to judge or to exercise spiritual authority.

called the Divine Office in which he prays in the name of the whole Church; 2nd to observe celibacy and continence; that is, not to marry and to preserve perfect purity of heart. St. Paul tells us:

"He that is without a wife, is solicitous for the things that belong to the Lord, how he may please God. But he that is with a wife, is solicitous for the things of the world, how he may please his wife: and he is divided." (I. Cor. VII. 32.)

The Latin Church thus imposes celibacy on her priests so that they may have no other family than that of the souls confided to their care; that they may be able to devote themselves exclusively to the service of these souls; and that they may be freer to consecrate themselves to every kind of ministry, whether in Christian or Pagan lands.

In such circumstances, therefore, it is only just that their material wants should be supplied by the faithful in accordance with the words of St. Paul. (I. Cor. IX.)

The first Catholic priests were St. Peter, who was Pope, the Apostles, who were bishops and those of the Faithful who were chosen and consecrated as priests and missionaries. Throughout the ages since the beginning of time this priesthood has been continued, and so it will be until the end of the world. When there are no longer priests, there will be no longer a Church, and so the world will come to an end.

CHAPTER XXXI

PENANCE

Contrition — Confession — Satisfaction — Indulgences — Sacramentals

BAPTISM effaces from the human soul every trace of sin, and causes to shine therein the light of supernatural life. But it does not change our nature, which always retains its evil inclinations; our free will remains, and if we commit a grave sin, we lose the life of grace and the friendship of God.

Who will restore it to us? Who will deliver us from remorse? Who will reopen to us the gates of Heaven?

Sincere sorrow for having offended God because He is God, the God who is infinitely great, infinitely Good, infinitely Holy, constitutes perfect Contrition, and can supply for Confession in cases where it would not be possible.

In all ages, this sincere sorrow for sin has been necessary to obtain pardon from God and to regain purity of heart, and it has always sufficed.

"I will arise," says the prodigal son in the Gospel, "and I will go to my Father." As soon as a sinner speaks thus from motives of perfect contrition, he is restored to the friendship of God; he is justified, but he is not dispensed from confessing his sins as Jesus Christ has ordained.

As no person can know whether he really has perfect contrition, our divine Lord has given us the Sacrament of Penance for the remittance of sins committed after Baptism to those who repent of them, confess them and make satisfaction for them.

Priceless blessing! What happiness, indeed, to have within our reach an easy and sure means of regaining peace of soul, the friendship of God, and the way of eternal salvation. In this world Catholics alone are assured of this.

To remit sins! God alone can do this, for He it is whom sin by destroying the order established by His will has offended; God alone, and consequently Jesus Christ in His character of God, of Redeemer, and of Mediator. Whilst on earth He did so directly when He pardoned Mary Magdalen, the Samaritan woman, the penitent Thief. But as He was about to disappear from amongst men on Ascension Thursday, He would communicate this power to those who were to replace Him on earth, until that day when He shall return "to judge the living and the dead."

This power is unlimited. There is no sin, no crime which cannot be remitted to him who repents sincerely — except the "sin against the Holy Ghost" — that is, final impenitence or the wilful obduracy of those about to die.

Our divine Lord instituted the Sacrament of Penance when He said to Peter and to the Apostles, and through them to the Popes, and through the Popes to the bishops and priests of the Catholic Church:

"Receive ye the Holy Ghost:

Whose sins you shall forgive, they are forgiven them; and whose sins you shall retain, they are retained." (St. John, XX. 22–23.)

Hence from Pentecost the Apostles, and after them, the bishops and priests have received the confessions of the Faithful and have remitted to them their sins (Acts, XIX. 18; St. James, V. 16; I. St. John, I. 9).

But in order to give or to refuse absolution for sins the priest must know them. And thus the sinner is bound to recall them, to declare them, to be sorry for them, to resolve not to commit them again, and to make atonement for them.

We must therefore:

First. Have for our past sins a sincere sorrow — this is what is called Contrition — and we must firmly resolve for the future not to commit them again — that is the Resolution. In other words we must simply be sincere with our conscience and with God. Perfect contrition, that which we feel because of having offended God, suffices in itself to wipe out all sin (we must have a fixed intention of going to Confession when possible); imperfect contrition, the sorrow we feel chiefly because of the punishment which by our sins we have merited, requires to be completed by the Sacrament of Penance.

Second. After having examined our conscience in order to discover the sins we have committed, we must confess them to a priest who has jurisdiction—that is who has received the necessary powers from his bishop, who has received them from the Pope, who has received them from Jesus Christ, to "loose and to bind," "to forgive and to retain," to give or to refuse absolution. This Confession, like our Contrition, must be true, sincere and complete—that is, it must, at least, include all mortal sins without exception.

Third. We must make satisfaction for our sins, which is done by saying what is familiarly called our "penance." The object of this "penance" is above all to make us feel the necessity of making reparation for the sins we have committed.

Contrition, Confession, and Satisfaction constitute the Sacrament of Penance.

This simple exposition enables us to see how

erroneous are the ideas which people sometimes form about this subject. For instance:

First. The Sacrament of Penance is not a human invention exploited by the Church for the purpose of obtaining power; it is a merciful means placed at our disposal by Jesus Christ, in order that men may be able to wash away their sins and tranquilize their consciences. How many non-Catholics would wish to make use of this means! Nay, the cases are not few of their actually addressing themselves to Catholic priests in the confessional and thus seeking relief for a burdened mind.

Second. No priest has of himself the power to forgive sins; this power belongs to God alone; but God exercises it through the ministry of the priest.

Third. It is equally inaccurate to say that for a Catholic to confess his sins suffices to obtain pardon of them. A confession made without sincere sorrow for sin and a firm resolution to amend is null and void.

Fourth. Although this Sacrament facilitates the obtaining of pardon for sin, it does not render sin the less hateful; still less is it an invitation to commit it again. On the contrary, it gives fresh energy to the will, and strengthens it with special grace to resist temptation.

But we are by no means asked to promise that

after having made our confession and received absolution we shall never again commit the same sin. Religion only imposes reasonable duties; she knows how weak human nature is, and only requires from it sincerity and good-will. All that religion asks of us is that when making our confession we should have sincere sorrow for our grave sins and firmly resolve to make use of proper means to correct them.

Sixth. Although confession does not make sin more easy, yet, on the other hand, those who dread confession are very wrong in thinking that it is a difficult and intolerable practise. If we had courage enough to offend God, we ought to have sufficient courage to make reparation; and it may be asserted that all those who purify their consciences by a good confession, find their reward in great consolation and happiness.

To the Sacrament of Penance or of the remission of sins are attached Indulgences and Sacramentals.

The word Indulgence signifies *a disposition to pardon, condonement, remission of a tax, of a debt, of a punishment*. In a religious sense it is the total or partial remission of the penalties or sufferings to which we are liable for our sins in this world or in the next, that is in Purgatory. In virtue of the powers which she has received from Jesus Christ the Church can grant this remittance to those who have the required dispositions (St. Matth. XVIII. 18). An indulgence is not therefore, as Protestants sometimes say it is, the remission of past sins nor of future sins, nor permission to sin nor a dispensation from eternal punishments—gross mistakes all or ridiculous inventions.

There are two kinds of indulgences:—a plenary indulgence which remits all punishment, and a partial indulgence which only remits part. Thus when we speak of an indulgence of 100 days, of 300 days, of seven years, this indulgence remits the penance which in the days of the early Christians we should have been obliged to perform during 100 days, 300 days, or seven years. These indulgences may be applied also to the souls in Purgatory, and they relieve their sufferings. To gain them: 1st. we must be in a state of grace, 2nd. we must comply exactly with the prescribed conditions.

"Jubilee" is a name given to a form of plenary indulgence which the Pope grants every twenty-five years and also on some other solemn occasions.

Finally, there are certain prayers, works, or holy objects which by the power of the Church have a particular effect, such as to lead us to God, to drive away from us all evil influences: these are called Sacramentals. Such are the ceremonies of the Church for those who devoutly assist at them; the devout use of holy water, which Catholics should always have in their homes in order to draw down upon them God's blessing and to drive away all contrary influences, the blessed ashes given on the first day of Lent, the Confiteor recited with the priest at the beginning of Mass; Alms given to the poor for the love of God, the religious instruction of the ignorant or of pagans, visiting the sick, the blessing of bishops and of priests.

Several of these good works are within our reach. Let us not neglect them; at the Last Day we shall reap the benefit of them.

CHAPTER XXXII

THE BLESSED EUCHARIST

Mass — Holy Communion [1]

THE word Eucharist (from the Greek εὐχαριστεῖν, to thank) signifies essentially "thanksgiving" rendered to God. It is, in effect, the most perfect act of thanksgiving, of adoration, of atonement, of supplication that can be, for it is Jesus Christ Himself Who makes this act — Jesus Christ risen from the dead, glorified and invisible, but really present and offering Himself as a sacrifice to God under the appearance of bread and wine. And for us it is also preeminently all joy, all grace, all good. It is the greatest gift which could be given to men. It is Emmanuel, "God with us."

We have considered the elements of the primitive religion. The central point of worship was the Sacrifice, still subsistent and recognizable in the forms of religion in the world under the mass

---

[1] Mass, from the Latin *missa*, (the act of dismissing after the Sacrifice). "Ite missa est" "Go; the Mass is over."

of superstition accumulated by time, ignorance or passion. Sacrifice was essentially an offering made by the head of the family or by the priest in the name of the people; an offering to the Divinity as an external manifestation of homage, of veneration, of adoration, with the intention of entering into relations with Him. Hence the sacrifice was not regarded as such until the offering was rendered useless to man; for this reason wine was spilled in libations, incense was burnt, and animals were slaughtered.

The sacrifices offered by Adam, Abel, Noe and the ancient Patriarchs were however but a figure of the great Sacrifice to come; they were to be replaced, and Malachias, the last of the Prophets, announced this emphatically to the Jews:

"Who is there among you, that will shut the doors, and will kindle the fire on my altar gratis? I have no pleasure in you, saith the Lord of hosts: and I will not receive a gift of your hand.

For from the rising of the sun even to the going down, my name is great among the Gentiles, and in every place there is sacrifice, and there is offered to my name a clean oblation: for my name is great among the Gentiles, saith the Lord of hosts." (Malachias, I. 10, 11.)

This "pure oblation" which was to be offered amongst all nations, is the divine Sacrifice of

Jesus Christ upon the Cross. Our divine Savior, representing as man the whole human race, by immolating Himself to God on Calvary acknowledged in Him the Sovereign Lord of the world and asked pardon of Him for the sins of the world. In other words the Man-God gave His life for the destruction of evil, the reparation of sin, and the renewal of the covenant with His Father and ours.

But our divine Savior was not satisfied with this. In order to apply to men individually the merits of this redemption, He has willed to institute Himself the holy Sacrifice of the Mass as the continuation and the unbloody representation of the Sacrifice of the Cross.

Long beforehand He had announced clearly this institution, as was His custom with the great events of His life. After having fed 5,000 people with five loaves and two fishes, He said to His disciples: "Amen, amen I say unto you: Except you eat the flesh of the Son of man, and drink his blood, you shall not have life in you. He that eateth my flesh, and drinketh my blood, hath everlasting life: and I will raise him up in the last day. For my flesh is meat indeed: and my blood is drink indeed. He that eateth my flesh, and drinketh my blood, abideth in me, and I in him." (St. John, VI. 54–57.)

A year later, on Holy Thursday, the eve of His

Passion and Death, our divine Lord assembled His twelve Apostles in the Cenacle to partake with them of the Pascal Lamb, figure of the Victim who was about to be immolated on Calvary. During the course of the supper Jesus took bread, and having blessed it, He broke it and distributed it saying: "Take ye, and eat: this is my body."

Then taking the chalice, He returned thanks to His Father, and giving it to His Apostles, He said:

"Drink ye all of this. For this is my blood of the new testament which shall be shed for many unto remission of sins." (St. Matth. XXVI. 26.)

And he charged His Apostles and their successors to do the same in memory of Him until the end of time.

Since then the Sacrifice of the Cross has been offered continually in all parts of the earth at every hour of the day, according as the sun rises in the different parts of the globe. Our divine Lord continues to dwell amongst men within reach of the greatest as well as the lowliest, and finally he permits those who desire to be really united by Holy Communion to His Sacrifice to participate in His divine life and to associate themselves with His all-powerful prayer.

By the institution of this Sacrament the Incarnation and the Redemption are daily renewed and continued amongst us. It is the incorporation of the Son of God with Humanity and of Humanity with the Son of God. What sublime mysteries! Truly such things could not be man's inventions.

Such is the Blessed Eucharist which Protestants have never been able to understand. How unspeakable their loss! That we are here in the presence of a great mystery is evident. But nothing can be clearer than the declaration with which it was instituted; to give them another meaning than that given by the Catholic Church is to say that Jesus Christ wished to deceive us.

Let us observe that there is no question here of a *transformation*, of replacing one form by another, but of a *transubstantiation*, of the mysterious real change of one substance into another substance. By virtue of the words of consecration, the substance of bread and wine is changed into the substance of the Body and of the Blood of Jesus Christ while the *species*, the impressions made on our senses, remain the same. Physical science, which is concerned with the properties of matter but which substance eludes, has no competence to decide on the possibility or impossibility of such a change: it belongs to another sphere.

We know moreover that obviously it is not the Body of our Lord in its natural state which dwells in the Blessed Eucharist under the appearance of bread and wine; it is His risen Body in its glorified state and not subject to the ordinary laws of nature. In this state, of which we know nothing, it takes the place of the bread and wine of which the species or appearances alone remain; and wherever may be found a fragment of the sacred Host or a drop of consecrated wine, our divine Savior is really present as Man and as God.

A comparison will help us to understand that this multiplied presence is not impossible. Expose a mirror to the rays of the sun, there in the mirror the sun is present. Break that mirror into a thousand fragments, the sun is in each one of them. It is in this sense that St. Augustine tries to give an idea of the mystery. "If I helped you," he says to his auditors, "to some material food, each of you could not receive the whole of it; I should divide it and the more numerous you were the less each of you would receive. It is not so with the Word of God, — each one receives it in its entirety. Now if such is the case with the human word, incarnate in a sound, why should not the Word of God incarnate in spiritual flesh be able to communicate Himself whole and entire under the appearance of bread and wine to every soul which receives Him?"

To sum up: the Blessed Eucharist is a Sacrament which contains truly, really, substantially, the Body, the Blood, the Soul and the Divinity of Jesus Christ under the appearances of bread and

wine for the spiritual nourishment of souls. The
Mass is the sacred rite during which the Eucharistic sacrifice is offered. Holy Communion is
the receiving of the Sacrament of the Eucharist.

Children as soon as they reach the use of reason
ought to receive Holy Communion, provided that
they have the necessary knowledge of what they
receive, and manifest sufficient moral dispositions
in the judgment of their parents and confessors.
After their first Communion all Catholics must
go to Communion at least once a year at Easter.
But to lead a holy life we should go to Holy Communion as often as possible. The conditions
under which we may do so are these only: — to be
fasting (that is to have taken nothing to eat or
to drink from midnight), to be unconscious of having committed mortal sin, to have a good intention
with a sincere desire to profit by Holy Communion
in becoming better. Those who are dangerously
ill are also obliged to receive Holy Communion;
but there is no obligation for them to be fasting;
the Communion thus received is called Viaticum,
that is, provision for their soul on its journey to
Eternity.

For the Christian, Holy Communion is a priceless blessing. By it we are united to our divine
Lord's life and love; it increases in us sanctifying
grace; it effaces the stains of sin; it diminishes
the force and the frequency of temptations; it

gives us greater vigor to resist evil; it consoles us in our trials; it is the true nourishment of our souls.

From a more general point of view what admirable lessons does not this divine institution teach all classes of society! What peace, what union, what humility, what resignation and charity result from it! By inviting all, the lowliest as well as the greatest, to the Eucharistic banquet our divine Lord reminds each one that before Him all men are equal. And after having been treated alike at this most magnificent of banquets, how can the poor envy the rich, how can the rich despise the poor?

CHAPTER XXXIII

THE SACRAMENT OF MATRIMONY

THE institution of Matrimony takes us back to the very beginning of humanity.

In the general plan of the Creation life created in the first organized beings — plants and animals — was transmitted to similar beings, who reproduce these and multiply them indefinitely, each one according to its species. It is the same with man whom God, says Holy Scripture, made to His own image by giving him an intelligent soul, and whom He created male and female.

And He blessed them and said to them: "Increase and multiply, and fill the earth, and subdue it, and rule over the fishes of the sea, and the fowls of the air, and all living creatures that move upon the earth." (Gen. I. 28.)

This is the origin of Marriage, of the Family and of Society.

Made for the transmission and the propagation of life in innocence, justice and holiness, Marriage has suffered much from the Fall of Adam and Eve. But it has kept the essential part of the

end for which it was first created; like Adam and
Eve, the father and mother of the human race,
husband and wife are united by marriage in a
community of life one and indissoluble, with the
holy mission of peopling the earth, and through
the earth Heaven also.

Man the guardian of life is thus associated with
the creative action of God; he calls into existence
beings endowed with understanding and capable
of calling in their turn others into life; he is the
purveyor of Heaven. How eminent the dignity
of parents!

Marriage by which the family is made and the
family by which Society is formed being of divine
institution, man cannot change their end or essential character. No doubt it belongs to the
State to protect marriage and the family by laws
regulating the temporal relations and interests of
husband and wife and of children; in this the
State is acting its proper part; but beyond this,
it must not go. Besides, human society was begun by marriage, not marriage by human society,
the latter therefore cannot claim the right to make
or to unmake the former.

Unhappily it has happened with marriage and
the family as with dogma and morals. According as the human race spread over the world, it
lost sight of the sanctity of the primitive institu-
tions, and, aided by passion, polygamy, divorce,

adultery, concubinage soon spread; all which abuses ruin the family, and by increasing, quickly destroy society itself. The ancient Patriarchs and the Jews did not altogether escape these evils, and the Mosaic Law under certain conditions permitted divorce and polygamy.

But when Jesus Christ came on earth, He restored marriage to its original purity, and made it a Sacrament of obligation for the Christian man and woman. The marriage law as God instituted it in the beginning, and as Christ restored it, consists in the union of one man with one woman, a union which the death of one or the other alone can dissolve. Cases, however, may arise in which husband and wife are permitted by the Church, as well as the civil law, to live apart; but the marriage endures, and neither the man nor the woman can contract another union.

The civil law of divorce established in some countries may take effect legally, but it cannot change the divine law. The divorced man or woman who contracts another union is not married; he or she lives in a state of continued sin, cannot approach the Sacraments, and so long as this union lasts, cannot be absolved. The law of divorce is not for Christians.

No doubt there are circumstances in which it may seem a hardship that marriage cannot be dissolved. But the happiness of individuals must yield to higher interests, and the education of children, the honor of conjugal society, the dignity of women, the purity of morals, the peace of families, and general morality — all these higher interests exact the stability of the marriage-tie.   A nation in which the family no longer counts will crumble to pieces.

But, it will be said; does not the Church herself dissolve certain marriages? — At the demand of one or other of the interested parties, the ecclesiastical tribunals consent, it is true, to examine the causes for the nullity of marriage referred to them.   If, after such examination, it is proved that the so-called marriage was null from the beginning — from want of consent, for example, — the decree of nullity is pronounced.   But where a marriage is validly contracted and confirmed by the conjugal act no power on earth can dissolve it afterwards.

Further, husband and wife are themselves the ministers of the sacrament; their free consent, expressed before the priest delegated to receive it, binds them for life by the matrimonial contract which for Christians is inseparable from the sacrament of Marriage; the two form but one and the same thing; and it would be an error to think that the sacrament is simply added to the contract as it were to complete it by a kind of religious sanction; one cannot be without the other;

without the contract there is no sacrament, and without the sacrament there is no marriage. Although husband and wife are the ministers of the sacrament, yet in order to safeguard morals in a matter of such importance, to assure the dignity of the contract and the general good of society, the Church has surrounded marriage with precautions and solemnities to which the faithful are bound in conscience to conform.

In the first place the Church has ordained that before marriage, there should be a promise of marriage given, an engagement entered into, which according to the religious law entails grave obligations and responsibilities.

Next the Church orders the proclamation of the banns in order that the projected marriage—a matter so intimately connected with the public welfare, should be made publicly known, and also that the discovery of impediments to the marriage — if any exist — may be facilitated.

Further, in the higher interests of morals the Church has fixed a certain number of *impediments*, of which some called *prohibitory* only concern the legality of the contract; others called *diriment* touch the very essence of the contract and render it null and void. To the latter category belong the *impediments* of consanguinity — relationship by blood — or affinity — relationship by marriage. Such relationships have been constituted *diriment impediments* in the moral and physical interests of families and races.

Hence no one should contract marriage without having first obtained from the Church a dispensation from all impediments which would affect the contract. The concealment of a diriment impediment would render the marriage contract radically null and void, and those guilty of such deception would be sure to suffer from the effects.

A marriage contracted without a condition of publicity required by the Catholic Church is called clandestine and invalid. By clandestine is meant secret, hidden, underhand; by invalid, that which does not hold good and is set aside.

The ecclesiastical impediment of clandestinity was first imposed by the Council of Trent (1545–1563) for sufficient reasons affecting the public good, and the security of marriage. This decree (*Tametsi*) declares every marriage clandestine and invalid, at which the Bishop or parish-priest of the man, or of the woman, is not present or another priest by his leave, or by the leave of the Bishop, together with at least two witnesses.

A later decree (*Ne temere*) of His Holiness Pius X. however has since modified the condition imposed by the Council of Trent. A marriage is now valid, as regards clandestinity, if celebrated in the presence of the parish Priest as above, or of the ordinary Priest of the place where the cere-

mony takes place, or in the presence of a priest
delegated by one or other of the aforesaid parochial authorities.

This law ceases to exist wherever the attendance
of a priest cannot possibly be produced or would
have to be waited for till a month had elapsed.
Then a solemn engagement before two witnesses
suffices.   Later the marriage must be entered on
the Parish or Mission registers.

In case of danger of death, the marriage may be
validly contracted before any priest assisted by
two witnesses whether he has been delegated or
not by the ecclesiastical authorities.

With regard to non-Catholics — baptized or
not — the Church regards the marriage of such
as valid, provided that none of the impediments
laid down by the divine law existed in the case of
either husband or wife.   This applies to divorced
persons.

Sometimes marriages are put off on the pretext
of want of means to pay the marriage fees.   No
priest has any right to refuse to perform or to
defer unreasonably the marriage ceremony for
such a reason.

The Church forbids the solemnization of marriage during the seasons of Lent and Advent but
in cases where delay is inadvisable a dispensation
can be obtained.

Such is Christian Marriage; a union which God

has willed and which by His Divine Providence forms the basis of all society, which is necessary to all civilization; a great and most holy institution by which weak human beings are, as it were, associated with the Creator in the propagation of the human race, in peopling earth, and in the conquest of ...ven.

Such is the exalted view which should be taken of the Sacrament of Marriage, and these are the sentiments which should animate all those who enter into the married state.

CHAPTER XXXIV

EXTREME UNCTION

I S any man sick among you," says the Apostle, St. James. "Let him bring in the priests of the church, and let them pray over him, anointing him with oil in the name of the Lord." (St. James V. 14.)

This is the Sacrament of Extreme Unction, that is, the anointing with holy oil, called *oleum infirmorum*, of the sick who are in extreme necessity or immediate danger of death. Extreme Unction is the Sacrament of the sick. When a person is unable to go to Confession, it supplies the place of the Sacrament of Penance, washes away the traces of sin, gives special graces to the dying, and if health is profitable for the sick person's salvation, this Sacrament contributes to its restoration. A priest alone can administer Extreme Unction, and it can only be received once during the same illness. Every Catholic who has come to the use of reason can receive this Sacrament even though unable to go to Confession.

In administering it, the priest makes with the

holy oil the sign of the Cross on the eyes, the ears, the nostrils, the lips, the hands, and feet of the sick person, praying God whilst he does so that God would wash away whatever sins may have been committed by means of each specified organ.

The last hours of life are also the most important; on them depends the lot of man for all eternity. This sacrament has been given to us as our last supreme aid: let us then not neglect it. Let us ask for it, and let us procure it for our dear ones who are ill; this is the greatest service we can render them in the last dread hours of life. Instead of having a bad effect upon them, experience proves that nothing so consoles them as the assurance of being at peace with God and prepared to appear before Him. Besides Extreme Unction has never yet killed any one, as superstitious or ignorant people are inclined to believe; on the contrary, it has helped to restore health to many. This indeed, we repeat, is one of its ends: to aid in the case of the sick if God should so will.

CHAPTER XXXV

Private Prayer — Public Prayer

TO pray to God, is to address ourselves to Him directly or indirectly; *to adore Him; to thank Him; to ask pardon of Him; to lay before Him our wants and our desires* for ourselves or for others, for the living or for the dead, for spiritual favors or for material goods. No doubt our sentiments and our poverty are known to God, but He wills, in prescribing prayer to us, as a father to oblige us to acknowledge our dependance on Him, and to preserve in us the respect, the gratitude and the love which we owe Him. Where is the child who would not speak to its father?

Let us pray; but let us pray with confidence, with humility, with perseverance. Prayer with the proper dispositions is certainly pleasing to God. True we do not always receive what we ask, nor immediately when we have asked. But does not God know better than we do what is good for us?

"You must always pray," says our divine Lord. To pray, it is by no means necessary to utter any words. Meditation and mental prayer are excellent forms of prayer. To work and to suffer whilst we keep ourselves in God's holy presence: that is prayer also. Thus understood, prayer is the simplest, the easiest, and the most general act of worship.

"You must always pray." To do our duty to the best of our power as the hours, the days, and the years pass away, keeping our conscience pure, our intentions upright, and our souls in peace: this is to pray always.

"Pray always." But let us each day devote some moments morning and evening to collect our thoughts in the presence of God. Family prayer, above all, is blessed by Heaven. What can be more touching than to see father, mother, children, servants, the whole household united in one and the same faith, one and the same attitude before Almighty God?

We address all our prayers to God through Jesus Christ, but we also have recourse to His Blessed Mother and to His friends, the Saints.

We distinguish between private prayer and public prayer. Private prayer is the prayer of individuals, public prayer is prayer offered in common, especially in the Church.

Not only did our divine Lord recommend prayer

to us both by word and example, but He willed to leave to men a formula of prayer—the Lord's Prayer,[1] which the better we understand it the more admirable we find.

"Our Father," how much this Name implies! It makes of all men as it were one immense family, all brothers, all dependent upon one another, to all of whom is allotted the same destiny. This prayer, so simple and so general, is indeed the prayer which is suited to the whole human race. God alone could give it to us.

Let us consider this prayer.

Our Father: Father of the great human family, the only Being to whom all creatures can give that name. Thou it is Who hast called us into life — natural and supernatural, Thou it is Who dost protect us: for us Thou hast spread, like a table always laid, the fruitful earth, and again beyond the gates of death Thou hast prepared for us a dwelling.

Who art in Heaven: Thou art undoubtedly everywhere, but it is in Heaven that Thou dost appear in all Thy glory; it is there that the Angels and Saints behold Thee; it is there that

---

[1] THE LORD'S PRAYER.

Our Father, who art in Heaven, hallowed be Thy name. Thy kingdom come; Thy will be done on earth as it is in heaven. Give us this day our daily bread; and forgive us our trespasses, as we forgive them who trespass against us; and lead us not into temptation, but deliver us from evil. AMEN.

one day the human family shall be united in Thee, in eternal peace.

Hallowed be Thy Name: Yes, let it be hallowed, glorified, and above all, known by all Thy children; by those who are consecrated to Thy special service; by priests; by religious; — by those who belong to Thee by Baptism and the practise of religion; by those who forget Thee; despise Thee; who offend, outrage Thee; who combat Thee; — by heretics, schismatics, apostates, infidels; by those who desire to go to Thee by the only ways they know; by those who know Thee not; by those who have never heard of Thee.

Thy Kingdom come. Reign Thou on earth by spreading everywhere the knowledge of truth and the practise of justice; reign Thou in our souls by developing therein supernatural life; reign Thou in Heaven by triumphing there with the ever-increasing number of the elect!

Thy Will be done on earth as in Heaven: As the Angels and Saints in Heaven will only what Thou willest, grant that we on earth may be ever submissive to the designs of Thy divine Providence in all things good and evil.

Give us this day our daily bread: We are in Thy Hands, and without Thee we can do nothing. Feed us, O Thou our Father, Who dost forget no one; this day feed our bodies, feed our souls;

to-morrow we shall once more stretch out our hands to Thee for the bread of our bodily life and that of our souls.

Forgive us our trespasses as we forgive them who trespass against us: We have sinned against Thee, but can we ask Thee to pardon us, if we ourselves cherish hatred and ill will against those who have offended us? Grant us forgiveness then, and forgive them.

Lead us not into temptation: We are often tempted; moved to evil; tried in many ways. Permit us not to yield to passion, to weakness, to discouragement. Permit not the light of Thy grace to be extinguished in our souls. Grant us Thy divine assistance.

But deliver us from evil: Above all, O Heavenly Father, deliver us from that bodily illness in all its forms which would prevent us from fulfilling the duties of our state in life, from illness of the soul which is sin, and from the supreme and irreparable evil which is eternal damnation.

Amen. O Heavenly Father, grant that it may be so, and hear this our poor prayer!

Another prayer dear to Catholics is the Hail Mary or Angelical Salutation.

Hail Mary, full of grace: As the Angel Gabriel saluted Thee, O Mary, I salute Thee, and have recourse to Thee, to Thee whose soul from the first moment of thine existence was filled with

CHAPTER XXXVI

THE HOLY SACRIFICE OF THE MASS

THE Mass is the great prayer of Catholic Worship.

In the primitive Religion and in the Mosaic Religion the Sacrifice was the central point of worship. In the Christian Religion which is the sequel and the end of the others, it is the same, only the Sacrifice surpasses them in grandeur and holiness beyond all that man could conceive.

Under the most common appearances — those of bread and wine, it is Jesus Christ Himself, Who having died upon the Cross for the redemption of mankind, mystically renews upon our altars that same sacrifice for our salvation. At the same time He gives Himself as mystical Food to the faithful that they may thus participate in His most pure sacrifice, may live His life and offer themselves with Him to the Supreme Lord of the Universe. Such is in effect the Holy Sacrifice of the Mass, during which, as foretold by the Prophet Malachy, a spotless victim is now offered to the Most High all over the whole inhabited world, according as the sun rises to spread

light and life. Since the day that the Creator
hid Himself in the earthly Paradise from Adam's
sight man has ever sought his God. The Mass,
which brings Jesus into our Churches, on our
Altars, into our Tabernacles, into our very hearts,
the Mass restores to man his God Whom he sought.
God is the life of all Catholic worship; He is the
Emmanuel,[1] He is "God with us." And this it is
which separates by such immeasurable distance
the Catholic Religion from Protestantism and all
other religions.

Similarly to the ancient sacrifices the Sacrifice
of the Mass is offered on an Altar or raised
stone by a priest who represents the whole assembled people and acts in their name. The
prayers, the singing, the ornaments, the sacerdotal
vestments, the sacred vessels, the rites and symbolic ceremonies—all should contribute to make
us understand that we are assisting in a more than
ordinary act; that it is indeed our divine Savior
Who in our presence and in union with us is offering Himself in sacrifice.

The priests' vestments, modified by time, are
those which were worn by priests in the first
ages of the Church in the Roman Empire. The
Alb is the *alba vestis* or *camissia*, still worn in the
East, the Stole (*stola*) is the border of the long
robe richly adorned which was worn by dignitaries;

[1] Emmanuel, a Hebrew word signifying, God with us.

the Chasuble is the *casula* or large vestment which covered the whole body; the dalmatic is a tunic originally worn by the Dalmatians; to these have been added the Amice (from *amicire*, to cover), white linen with which the neck is covered; the Maniple, formerly only a handkerchief, worn on the left arm; the Girdle used to tighten the alb.

According to the ceremonies which accompany it, the Mass is a High Mass with deacon and sub-deacon, a *Missa cantata* (sung Mass) or a Low Mass.

To say Mass is of obligation for priests only on those occasions when the faithful are bound to be present — namely, Sundays and holidays of obligation. The Church, however, authorizes them and exhorts them to celebrate Mass every day. On Christmas Day and on the Feast of All Souls (2nd Nov.) the priest has power to celebrate three Masses; on Sundays and holidays of obligation, when necessary to supply the religious needs of the people, he may say two. The priest must be fasting, and Mass can be celebrated only during the hours between dawn and mid-day. On Sundays and holidays, the priest who has charge of souls (for instance, the Parish Priest) offers Mass for his parishioners; on all other days he may offer it for private intentions.

Offerings for Masses are offerings made by persons, according to custom, when they request the celebration of the Holy Sacrifice for some special intention, not by way of recompense for the Mass itself which is of infinite value, but as an act of gratitude and a small contribution established by the Church and necessary for the support of her ministers.

From the earliest ages of Christianity the Mass has been divided into two parts; the first part which was called the Mass of the Catechumens,[1] because those who were not yet baptized could be present only during it, and the Sacrifice properly so called, or the Mass of the Faithful. The first part after the preparatory prayers at the foot of the Altar comprises the Introit,[2] the invocation of the Kyrie Eleison,[3] the Gloria in Excelsis Deo, said or sung by the priest, the Collects, then an extract from the Epistles of the Apostles, then an extract from the Gospels, and lastly the Credo, which is the summary of our Faith.

The second part of the Mass comprises the Offertory, or offering of the bread and wine, the Consecration, at which the priest pronounces the sacred words by which the bread and the wine are changed into the Body and Blood of our divine

[1] Catechumens, those who are prepared for Baptism.
[2] Introit, that is, entrance.
[3] Kyrie Eleison, Greek words, signifying, Lord, have mercy on us.

Savior, and lastly, the Communion which is the consummation of the Sacrifice.

In the early ages of Christianity, all those present joined with the priest in receiving Holy Communion, and we are invited to do the same. At least let us make an Act of spiritual communion by uniting ourselves to Jesus Christ, by our desire of receiving Him, our sorrow for our sins, and our sincere will to serve Him.

When we understand it, how great, how beautiful is Holy Mass!

The priest is at the Altar offering to God the holiest of sacrifices in the name of the people whom he represents, and of whom he is the recognized and consecrated intermediary. Behind him and united with him in his prayers are the congregation, all marked by Baptism which makes them Christians and adopted children of God.

And from all these prayers results a great consolation—that of feeling oneself united through time and space with all one's friends, living and dead, in the same faith, the same hopes, even to eternity. This is the magnificent communion of the faithful realized in the communion in the same sacrifice. This is equality before God. This is social union realized in the same faith, the same love, the same hopes.

CHAPTER XXXVII

THE LITURGICAL YEAR

THE religious or liturgical year is so arranged as to recall to us by a regular cycle of feasts and solemnities God's action in the world, to revive for us the life of Jesus Christ, and to glorify Him in His saints.

This liturgical year begins on the first Sunday of Advent.[1] The season of Advent is of four weeks' duration, and carries us back to the long ages which preceded the coming of our divine Savior. Then comes the season from Christmas to Ascension Thursday which recalls to us the thirty-three years of our Lord's life on earth, and during which we try to live in His life; at Christmas by assisting at his birth; at the Epiphany [2] by adoring Him with the Magi; during Lent by doing penance with Him; on Palm Sunday and during Holy Week, by following Him in His Passion; at Easter by glorifying Him in His Resurrection, and later in His Ascension.

[1] Advent, arrival, coming.
[2] Epiphany — manifestation (of Jesus to the world).

Finally in that portion of the year which is included between Pentecost and Advent, we see the Holy Ghost taking possession of the Catholic Church and multiplying for souls the means of salvation. It is during this time that the Feasts of the Holy Trinity, Corpus Christi and the Sacred Heart are celebrated. Thus Catholic Worship embraces all times, having for its sole object God, the Father, the Son, and the Holy Ghost. And as God is everywhere in it, so also is Jesus Christ. Whilst we recall the principal phases of His earthly life, He is with us in the living reality of the Blessed Eucharist, He it is, so to say, who presides at our Festivals.

Many generations have gone before us to Him, and many will follow us. As in our turn we pass before Him who endures, prostrate we adore Him, afterwards to give place to others, and to enter into our eternity. Such is the grand sequence of Catholic worship.

CHAPTER XXXVIII

OUR CHURCHES

IN all ages Religion has dedicated to divine worship holy places or sanctuaries where the people assembled round the priest to hold communion with God; to offer Him homage and sacrifice. When the Israelites were journeying to the Promised Land, Moses caused a Tabernacle to be made, that is a kind of large tent which served as a place of prayer. Later, after the conquest of the Holy Land this ambulant tabernacle was replaced by a magnificent temple built by Solomon in Jerusalem in the year 1004 B.C. Destroyed by the Babylonians and subsequently rebuilt, this temple was finally destroyed by the Romans in the year of our Lord 70; since that time the Jews have had no temple, only synagogues or "places of meeting" for prayer; in these no sacrifice has ever been offered.

The first Christians in the beginning met in private dwellings, and even sometimes in subterranean chambers which served them as cemeteries — since called catacombs. But as soon as

278

the persecutions ceased in the Roman Empire under Constantine (315) they assembled in special buildings which, being blessed or consecrated for divine worship, could not be used for any other purpose.

A Church, which is often built in the form of a cross, comprises the choir reserved for the clergy, and the nave or body for the faithful.

Church furniture consists, in the first place, of the altar or altars on which is offered the Holy Sacrifice. On one of these altars is placed the tabernacle in which the ciborium containing the consecrated Hosts is reserved. Before the tabernacle or beside it burns perpetually the lamp of the Blessed Sacrament which represents the faithful before our Lord and burns away in His presence like a never ending prayer. Then there are the Communion-rails at which our Lord gives Himself to us to be the food of our souls; the pulpit in which His Word is preached to us; the confessional in which our sins are remitted. At the entrance of the Church is the baptistery or baptismal font at which we are made Christians. For the sacred functions are used the sacred vessels — the chalice; the paten; the ciborium; monstrance, etc.; the Altar-linen; liturgical ornaments and vestments; and certain natural products, such as incense, which is used as a sign of prayers and adoration ascending like a sweet perfume to God; the lights which are the symbol of faith and charity.

In the first centuries the vestments were made of linen or of white silk; now they must be made of silk. Later the four liturgical colors now used were established; *White* worn on Feasts of our Lord, of our Lady, of Confessors, etc.; *Red* at Pentecost and on the Feasts of Martyrs; *Green* on all Sundays; *Violet* in penitential seasons, Advent, Lent, etc. At offices for the Dead, *Black* is used. Every detail of divine Worship in the celebration of the various offices and the administration of the Sacraments has been regulated according to the liturgy, the collection of symbolic rites and ceremonies consecrated by the authority of the Church and the venerated usage of past ages.[1]

Fundamentally the Catholic liturgy is everywhere the same, being as it is the external expression of one and the same belief, of one and the same morality; but in the ceremonies, the languages employed, etc., it permits of various modes of expression. Hence the general difference in the liturgies of the Churches of the East and West. The liturgies of the former comprise the Liturgy of Jerusalem whence came the Maronite rite used by the Christians of Lebanon in which is used the Syriac tongue (Syriac was the language spoken in Judea in the time of our Lord); then the Armenian

---

[1] Liturgy, from the Greek, λειτουργία, public service.

liturgy; those of the Greek Melchites, of the Syrians, of the Chaldeans, of the Slavs or united Bulgarians.

In the Church of the West the Roman liturgy is the principal one; it is also called the Gregorian rite from the Pope, St. Gregory the Great, who in the sixth century codified it according to traditions handed down from St. Peter and Apostolic times. In this liturgy, which is ours, the Church has retained the use of the Latin language, the language in which the Gospel was preached in Rome. The advantage of this is that Latin being now what is called a dead language, is no longer subject, as are living languages, to perpetual changes. Besides, in this way Catholic unity is better maintained, while the international relations of the Church with the entire world are facilitated by the use of one language only.

All religions have centers for meeting places of worship, temples — buildings more or less beautiful, sometimes even splendid. But the Catholic Church alone has living temples, and with what life are they alive! In them burns the lamp of the Sanctuary, and in them reposes the Blessed Sacrament; Christ dwells in them, as He has said, amongst the children of men. It is this which gives to our churches, no matter how humble they may be, a distinctive and unique character. The most unhappy as well as those most favored by fortune can there hold communion with Jesus Christ. If their hearts are pure, their souls righteous, He will hear them and they will hear Him.

What unspeakable honor, what ineffable happiness and consolation it is for Catholics to have in their midst their churches wherein dwells their God, their divine Redeemer, their Judge!

It is because of this that we love our Churches so much; in them we are in our home.

CHAPTER XXXIX

CONCLUSION

LET us sum up and let us conclude.

If God does not exist, man is truly incomprehensible, and not only man, but the whole world, the smallest insect, the least blade of grass, all that lives, all that moves, all that is, becomes incomprehensible. God is the necessary being; sane reason exacts that for all the beings we see around us there must be a first, eternal Cause. Without this cause, nothing can be explained.

But if God is, He is evidently superior to all, infinitely just, infinitely good. He could not have created men except that they might know Him and love Him. Now, if in His mercy, in spite of their weakness, their errors and their sins, He has called them to share His life, He must give them the means of attaining to it.

If He has willed that there should be such accumulated proofs of the divinity of Jesus Christ, it is because Jesus Christ is God and the messenger of God to man.

If Jesus Christ is God and God's Messenger to men, the Catholic Church which He left after Him is divine. He has given to man that which He promised. Now, since He said that He would be with the Church until the end of time, the way in which we should go has been marked out for us; we have but to follow the Church in the teaching which she gives us, as in the law which she imposes on us.

But did Jesus Christ found the Catholic Church such as she is at the present day? Yes; He has founded and willed and proclaimed her to be the one, true and universal society with a Head to Whom He has given power and authority to organize her. To the Church He has confided the deposit of the Faith; He has ordained her to preach the Gospel to all nations. He has promised to be with her until the end of time. The Roman Catholic Apostolic Church as she is now, is the Church of Christ — unless we admit what is inadmissible — that Christ in His work has failed miserably.

No doubt there is obscurity; there are difficulties and objections. But, first of all — is it our place to advise God as to the religious organization to be given to mankind? What are we, and who is God? If there is obscurity, is it not to render our faith meritorious? If there are difficulties, is it not to oblige us to make efforts?

If there are objections, is it not that we may be led to seek the light and to confess the truth bravely? And is it a matter for surprise that our understanding, weak as it is, when it seeks to search into the Essence of God and of His Providence should meet with unfathomable mysteries such as are met with so often in natural phenomena?

To all the objections urged against her for twenty centuries, the Catholic Religion — extraordinary and unexampled — has ever given a triumphant answer. Only those who have not listened to her or who have not understood her, believe that she is powerless to reply to her detractors.

Moreover, can it be admitted that all that humanity has produced throughout the ages of what is purest, most devoted, most enlightened and virtuous, could be in what concerns religious truth, victims of the grossest delusion, by laboring for empty hopes, by making their life's goal of nothingness?

The problem of evil itself, of sorrow, of error, of injustice, however painful to those who suffer, becomes the surest ground of our hopes. Of necessity there must be another life in which we are indemnified for all, in which all is explained.

Finally, in practise, there is one argument which must carry weight. If by an impossibility, there exists nothing of what we believe, neither soul nor God, neither Heaven nor Hell; if everything in the world is the result of chance, and if all must end in eternal night, at least by living as a Christian, I shall have lived the worthiest, the most useful, the most consoling of lives, in the peace of a good conscience and with comforting support of immortal hopes.

And if, as everything proves to us, the Catholic Religion gives to us in Heaven all that she promises, what ineffable happiness for believers! But what an awakening in the land beyond the grave for the wilfully, criminally impious, for those who are indifferent, for the cowardly; what a fearful deception, what irreparable ruin!

I have decided which side I shall take. I am for God and His Christ for time and for eternity. I am a Catholic.

CHAPTER XL

PRACTICAL ORGANIZATION OF THE CHRISTIAN LIFE

TO study Religion; to seek the truth; to make for oneself a reasonable faith; to examine that one may believe: all this is necessary. But, let us repeat it, by the grace of God alone is the gift of Faith and the practise of Faith received. And only humble submission of the understanding, simplicity of heart, sincerity, repentance, good-will, prayer, will obtain the grace of God. Once we have recognized the truth, let us accept it wholly and no matter what it may cost us, with all its consequences and all that it exacts; this is strictly required of us.

Our first thought—the one which must ever dominate all others, is by the possession of divine grace to enter into the supernatural life, to maintain ourselves in it, to die in it.

We can secure this for ourselves by Baptism, and should we afterwards lose the baptismal grace, by Penance.

The Christian life of grace must be maintained

and sustained by the faithful observance of the Commandments of God and of the Church, by frequenting the Sacraments, by the faithful fulfilment of the duties of one's state of life; the whole being based on the great virtues, natural and supernatural, of justice, of truthfulness and fidelity, of moral energy, of the complete and generous accomplishment of duty.

If faults, even grave faults, reappear, we must never be discouraged. The Sacraments have been given to us as so many fountains in which the soul may be purified, nourished and fortified.

Learn to know and understand your religion. Never regard as final any objection which may be urged against it. The Catholic Church has an answer for every objection; she will certainly have one for any that may arise to give you trouble.

Nevertheless, we have no right to expose our faith to temptation. Do not read irreligious or immoral books, reviews or papers; do not allow them into your house.

Work — even if you are not obliged to do so for the support of yourself or of those belonging to you. No one, but above all no Christian worthy of the name, has a right to lead a useless life.

In accordance with your capabilities and your tastes, with your circumstances and necessities, order your life judiciously in the view of your eternal destiny, and keep firmly to your good resolutions.

Be resigned in sufferings. Hope ever. And thus in spite of the disappointments, the trials, and the afflictions of which you may have your share, you will experience the truth of those words of Pascal: "No one is so happy as a true Christian."

ALPHABETICAL INDEX

A

Abraham, 59, 63, 220.

Absolution, 240, 243.

Abstinence (Law of), 193.

Actions (human), 146.

Adam, 43.

Adoration duty of, 162, 163.

Adultery, 179.

Advent, 276.

All Saints, 189.

Altar, 275, 279.

Angels, 41; worship of, 220.

Anger, 156.

Anti-Christ, 130.

Apostasy, 154.

Apostles, choosing of the, 67; mission of the, 79-80.

Ascension, 189

Assumption, 189.

Authority of the Church, 104.

Avarice, 156.

B

Banns, publication of, 258.

Baptism, 228; of desire, 230; of blood, 231.

Baptismal vows, 229.

Belief, Catholic, 29.

Betrothal, 258.

Bible, 18; the Church and the, 101.

Bishops, 99-100.

Blasphemy, 167.

C

Calumny, 184.

Catholic Belief, 79.

Catholics (statistics), 121, 122.

Celibacy of priests, 237; of Religious, 202.

Charity, 155, 156.

Chastity, 179; vow of, 202.

Children (duties of), 171.

Christ (predicted), 59. See Jesus.

Christianity (comes from God), 84; social rôle, 116-117. See Church.

Catholics, 119; number of, 122.

Christmas, 189.

Church, Catholic, 11; has the Deposit of the Faith, 15; only Rule of our Faith, 96, 101; its definition, 97; its Head, 98; Roman, 99, 109; Hierarchy of the Church, 100; marks of the, 104; weaknesses of the, 106; attacks against the, 107; progressive advance of the Church, 125; Church and State, 209-210; Mission of the, 114; social

291

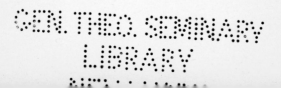